Faith Confronts Evil

Faith Confronts Evil

*From Birthmothers to Holy Women,
African American Christian Women, 1619–1865*

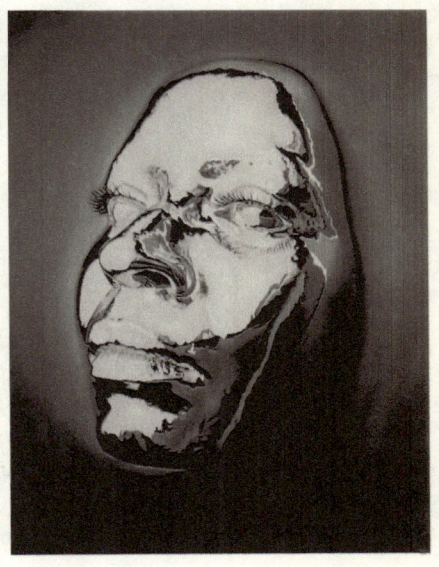

Barbara Omolade
with Susan M. Felch

Afterword by Willie James Jennings

 CASCADE *Books* · Eugene, Oregon

FAITH CONFRONTS EVIL
From Birthmothers to Holy Women, African American Christian Women, 1619–1865

Copyright © 2024 Barbara Omolade. All rights reserved. Except for brief quotations in critical publications or reviews, no part of this book may be reproduced in any manner without prior written permission from the publisher. Write: Permissions, Wipf and Stock Publishers, 199 W. 8th Ave., Suite 3, Eugene, OR 97401.

Cascade Books
An Imprint of Wipf and Stock Publishers
199 W. 8th Ave., Suite 3
Eugene, OR 97401

www.wipfandstock.com

PAPERBACK ISBN: 978-1-6667-7794-9
HARDCOVER ISBN: 978-1-6667-7795-6
EBOOK ISBN: 978-1-6667-7796-3

Cataloguing-in-Publication data:

Names: Omolade, Barbara, author. | Felch, Susan M., author. | Willie James Jennings, afterword.

Title: Faith confronts evil : from birthmothers to holy women, African American Christian women, 1619–1865 / Barbara Omolade with Susan M. Felch.

Description: Eugene, OR: Cascade Books, 2024 | Includes bibliographical references and index.

Identifiers: ISBN 978-1-6667-7794-9 (paperback) | ISBN 978-1-6667-7795-6 (hardcover) | ISBN 978-1-6667-7796-3 (ebook)

Subjects: LCSH: African American women—History. | Slavery—United States—History. | African American women—Religious life.

Classification: E185.86 O40 2024 (paperback) | E185.86 (ebook)

VERSION NUMBER 10/22/24

Front cover art: *Diovadiova Chrome Karyn III* © Kip Omolade, 2023. All rights reserved. Used with permission.

For my children and their families, with
thanks for God's greatest blessings.
Barbara Omolade

For Doug, with thanks for fifty years of ministry together.
Susan M. Felch

Contents

Preface | ix
Acknowledgments | xiii
Introduction | xv

1. The Birthmothers: An Evil beyond Toil and Torture | 1
2. The Road to Conversion | 19
3. Phillis Wheatley: Christian Oracle | 33
4. Hope and Despair in the New Nation | 51
5. Hell Without Fires: The Second Middle Passage | 63
6. Prayer Warriors and Spiritual Warfare | 77
7. The Holy Women: Sojourner Truth and Harriet Tubman | 89
8. The Holy Women Fight for Freedom | 105

Afterword: The Work of Hope by Willie James Jennings | 125
In Memory of Dr. Barbara Jones Omolade | 129
Bibliography | 133
Index | 137

Preface

FAITH CONFRONTS EVIL is a tale of two stories.

The first story is the one told in this book: an account of African American Christian women who lived before the Civil War and for whom Christian faith was central to how they lived and how they understood themselves.

The second story is that of two authors, one African American and one white, whose long friendship and shared Christian faith propelled this book into print.

The second story began in June 1999 when Barbara Omolade and Susan Felch met at Calvin College (now Calvin University) in Grand Rapids, Michigan. Susan was directing a Faculty Summer Seminars program, and Barbara was joining the God and Evil Seminar led by Peter van Inwagen, a philosopher from Notre Dame.

Barbara came to the seminar with impressive academic credentials. She held a PhD in sociology from the City University of New York and was a professor of African American and women's studies at City College of New York. She had already published *The Rising Song of African American Women* (Routledge, 1994) and was well regarded as an educator and administrator. Barbara had an equally impressive history as an activist in women's and civil rights movements, beginning with her participation in the Student Nonviolent Coordinating Committee from 1962 to 1966 and continuing with leadership roles in various organizations, including the Women's Action Alliance and the Sisterhood of Black Single Mothers. Documents from the former organization are archived in the Barbara Omolade Papers (RG 15.7) at Sarah Lawrence College. Although Barbara had attended church as a child, she drifted away from the faith until middle age, when she experienced the power of conversion and became a born-again Christian.

Preface

As she traveled throughout the United States and saw believers grappling with issues of racism and diversity in both small and large churches, she recognized they lacked historical context and knowledge of the formation of Christianity in the United States and the roots of the African American faith tradition. Hence, her interest in the God and Evil Seminar.

Susan joined the English department at Calvin College in 1992, after receiving her PhD from The Catholic University of America in Washington, DC, and began directing the Summer Seminars program in 1997. As a third-culture kid who had grown up in Papua New Guinea, she resonated with Barbara's global experiences, including her year on an Israeli kibbutz and travels to China, Belize, and England, and their shared perspective on the complexities of cross-cultural encounters both internationally and within the North American context. Their social science and humanities training, as well as their gender, made them a minority among the male philosophers who largely populated the seminars, and they soon found other common interests, as well. Among these was a firm desire to promote faithful living, teaching, and scholarship within the academy, and to do so within the Christian vision of a community where women and men from every kindred, tongue, people, and nation worship and serve the Lord God (Rev 5:9, KJV).

One outgrowth of their friendship was Barbara's appointment in 2003 to become the first dean for multicultural affairs at Calvin College. During Barbara's tenure as dean, which was unfortunately shortened due to health complications, she and Susan strengthened their personal friendship as they continued to work together professionally.

Another outgrowth, which began even before Barbara became dean, was the establishment of a Consultation of African American Christian Scholars, a week-long seminar held annually at Calvin University from 2001 to 2005. Barbara and Susan co-directed the first seminar, but thereafter Susan ceded her role to Dr. Willie Jennings (now at Yale Divinity School). The consultation was designed to bring together African Americans who self-identified as Christian scholars, so that they could encourage and strengthen one another in their academic vocations. Both Barbara and Susan realized that these scholars, who usually worked in majority white institutions, faced challenges that were often overlooked or misunderstood by their colleagues. The consultation provided a space for African American scholars to articulate their particular experiences and to strengthen the gifts they brought to Christian higher education. From the start, participants recognized that although all scholars, religious or secular, Black or white, male or female, share a commitment to a "life of the mind," they do not share the same relationship to the social, cultural, and institutional structures that frame and express that life. Making visible those different relationships was one goal of the consultation, along with creating a supportive community with a shared voice that was not oppositional to, but was certainly distinctive from, the majority white cast of Christian scholarship in the early twenty-first century.

The consultation took as its founding motto the words in the opening editorial of *Freedom's Journal*, the first African American owned newspaper (1827): "We wish to plead our own cause. Too long have others spoken for us. Too long has the public been deceived by misrepresentations, in things which concern us dearly." In pleading their own cause, the consultation participants did not turn away from institutions of Christian higher education in North America, but rather sought to be a faithful voice within those institutions by offering a fuller perspective on the formation of Christian witness, education, and scholarship in the United States, thus correcting misrepresentations and strengthening faculty to move forward with a robust Revelation 5 vision.

"We wish to plead our own cause" also provides an important motivation for this book. Since her retirement from Calvin College, Barbara has continued her research into the founding stories of the Christian faith in North America, with a particular focus on the under-told stories of African American women before the Civil War. Together, Barbara and Susan have become convinced that these stories should be more widely known and acknowledged as integral to the history of the United States, as well as to the history of Christianity. The best way to tell these stories is to let African American women of the past plead their own cause.

Of course, there may be resistance to these stories. Young African American students and some scholars may think that Christianity is now irrelevant to current struggles for equity and inclusion and that its history is hopelessly compromised by the institution of slavery. Young white students, and students of color outside the African American community, may think that any form of African American history is irrelevant to their own lives. Older Americans are often quite ignorant of the multiple strands that constitute their own history and regard focus on a particular strand as unnecessary, divisive or, again, irrelevant.

Preface

What we have learned over the course of our long friendship and collaboration is that stories, truthfully told, are never irrelevant. Shared stories are what turn strangers into acquaintances, acquaintances into friends, colleagues into collaborators. The stories of antebellum African American Christian women is our story, whether that "our" embraces those who self-identify as Christians or those who are merely interested in the early formation of the United States.

The stories told in this book are saturated with belief in, and the language of, the Christian faith. Although many think that Christianity brainwashed and crushed the agency of enslaved Africans, it actually had the opposite impact. Many African Americans came to view Christianity as a faith of liberty, humanity, and justice in which God was on their side, Jesus was their friend, and the Holy Spirit was their guide to all truth. Faith provided African Americans with validation of their humanity and reinforced their claims for liberty. For African Americans, Christianity and political freedom became an interwoven social force that lasted until the mid-twentieth century. African American Christians who for so long struggled to plead their own cause also always highlighted and pled the cause of Jesus.

As we have worked on this book, both of us have been strengthened in our own lives as we have witnessed the courageous Christian witness of our mothers in the faith. The title of this book is *Faith Confronts Evil*, not *Evil Confronts Faith*, and the order of the nouns is significant. Despite the rampant evil of slavery, the words of the gospel, that Jesus comes to set the captives free, resounds through all these stories. Faith confronts evil and it triumphs, even in death. This is the good news we all—from every kindred, tongue, people, and nation—need to hear.

Acknowledgments

THIS BOOK HAS BEEN many years in the making. We thank the Calvin Center for Christian Scholarship and its then director, James D. Bratt, for funding the Consultation of African American Christian Scholars, and we appreciate all those who participated in that yearly seminar. We especially thank Willie James Jennings for co-directing the consultation, for his warm personal friendship over the years, and for his advice on this book at critical junctures. We also thank the editors at Cascade Books for their attentiveness, especially Matthew Wimer, who answered many questions with grace and efficiency.

I (Barbara) would like to recognize my personal support system, "The Fourteen": My four children, Kip, Ngina, Eskimo, and Krishna, their spouses Diana and Ghislain, and my eight grandchildren, Genese, James, Jonathan, Trevor, Addie, Kent, Kace, and Sky. Kip painted the portrait that appears on the cover; Ngina has managed publication details and provided stalwart prayer support; Eskimo and especially Krishna have taken care of my daily needs. I would like to thank my pastor, Rev. Jamar Jackson, and my church family at Metropolitan United Methodist Church in Princess Anne, Maryland for their fellowship and support. I also want to thank my sister in Christ, Susan Felch, whose editing and diligent work enabled this project to be completed.

I (Susan) thank Barbara and her family for inviting me to join them in bringing *Faith Confronts Evil* to publication. As always, my deepest thanks is to my husband, Doug, who takes care of me, the house, and our cats as I write.

We are both grateful for our friendship over many years. We praise God for the strength he has provided to tell the story of Christian women

Acknowledgments

who overcame tremendous hardship through faith in Christ. We are humbled to stand with them, looking unto Jesus the author and finisher of our faith (Heb 12:2, KJV).

Introduction

ON MARYLAND'S EASTERN SHORE, a woman lifts a mike and sings "Faithful, Faithful Is My God." In Brooklyn, New York, two women in an apartment church sing worship songs they have composed. In a midwestern church, a woman worship leader sings "He Knows My Name." In a church in Georgia, a woman sings "In His Presence." On any Sunday morning in the United States, African American Christian women can be found in churches worshipping God in song. These women are keepers of a tradition as old as the United States itself, based on the belief that faith can confront and vanquish social evil. This faith tradition has defined African American Christian women's faith and resistance to social evil, inspired their music, and sustained their families and communities from the antebellum era to the present.

The roots of slavery and the racism these women faced started at the cross, where the Bible says there were women who witnessed Christ's suffering. It continued later at the cave where they joyfully confirmed his resurrection. Like those women, enslaved African American women were daily witnesses to Christlike suffering, but they also rejoiced with the risen Christ. The faith of African American women was born amid the dark abodes of slavery when Christ was revealed as a kinsman-redeemer, not a white master.

African American women first heard the gospel from the white Christians in colonial America who owned and abused them. Their own faith, however, upended the aims of those white Christians who endorsed slavery and believed conversion could be used to suppress their slaves' courage and resistance. Though taught by their owners the "biblical mandate" that servants must obey their masters, the enslaved also heard, "For as many of you as have been baptized into Christ have put on Christ. There is neither Jew nor Greek, there is neither bond nor free, there is neither male nor female: for ye are all one in Christ Jesus" (Gal 3:27–28, KJV).

Away from the eyes of their owners and overseers, enslaved women became prayer warriors and a cloud of witnesses over their people, praying for freedom. Although faith has neither gender nor race, faith was distinctly expressed and understood by women who defied and served their evil owners and kept believing though enslaved.

Faith Confronts Evil documents the interplay between the evil social order and the women's faith that confronted and vanquished the powerful slave regime that held them and their children in bondage. This is a historical work of social analysis within a religious paradigm. It is a narrative based on the words and deeds of African American Christian women, whose faith became the foundation for the churches attended by so many today. Although the focus is on women, *Faith Confronts Evil* also explores the larger context in which Christianity flourished among enslaved and free African Americans.

During the earliest decades as a colonial society, enslaved women and girls brought from Africa the only things they were allowed to carry: sounds of worship and moans of despair. They became Birthmothers to African Americans by enduring an evil beyond toil and torture that birthed enslaved children fathered by European, Native American, and African men. Birthmothers and their children became essential to the nation's wealth with its race-based slave regime that lasted from 1619 to 1865.

Faith Confronts Evil tells the story of these women and the contexts in which they lived. Wherever possible, it uses their own words, so that we may hear their voices for ourselves. It also tells the larger story of slavery in the United States and lets us hear the voices of enslaved women, men, and children raised against abuse and for freedom.

1

The Birthmothers

An Evil beyond Toil and Torture

> *For the eyes of the Lord are over the righteous,*
> *and his ears are open unto their prayers:*
> *but the face of the Lord is against them that do evil.*
>
> —1 Pet 3:12, KJV

The history of African American Christian women begins with the stories of Birthmothers. These women gave birth to the families and communities that became the foundation of African American life. They were the hopeful survivors of an evil beyond toil and torture.

The first generation of Birthmothers were born in Africa. They were women and girls who were first bought or kidnapped from their villages by African merchants. Then they were marched to European trading "factories" and plantations on the coast. But their suffering was only beginning. Soon they were forced aboard ships bound for America, where they endured the terror and horror of the Middle Passage. The Middle Passage was the trans-Atlantic voyage between Africa and the Americas that permanently separated enslaved Africans from their own mothers and their motherland. Although the slave trade was intended to make a profit, the seven-to-eight-week Middle Passage was a questionable business venture.

So many millions of enslaved Africans died from violence and disease that it has been called "a holocaust at sea." Aboard the ships, boys and men were chained together and packed into cargo holds. The women and girls moved unshackled on the decks, but they were subjected to routine sexual abuse by the seamen. These Birthmothers came from different regions, cultures, and tribes in Africa. They held different religious beliefs. But during the Middle Passage, they prayed to the same all-knowing and all-powerful God for protection and deliverance from their condition and unknown fate.

The Birthmothers arrived in the North American colonies along with the British settlers. After their arrival, the captured Africans, who were tied together by a common motherland and horror-filled journey, were suddenly separated. They were sent to settler farms many miles apart or to newly built plantations. Small groups of slaves sometimes were sold together, but more often the African woman or girl now found herself without family on some New England farm, southern field, or in a rough cooking area in the woods. The Africans around her probably did not speak her language or dialect, nor did she understand her owner's English language. She was soon to learn the harsh realities of living in a New World.

Birthmothers in Virginia

Birthmothers arrived in Jamestown, Virginia, the first permanent English settlement in North America, within the first dozen years after its founding in 1607. They were suddenly transplanted into a newly settled area filled with pine forests, rivers, and Native American nations, very unlike their African homeland. Jamestown itself was named for King James VI, whose charter to the Virginia Company of London encouraged the settlers to bring Christianity to those who "as yet live in darkness and miserable ignorance of the true knowledge and worship of God."[1]

Despite this charter, Jamestown was more business enterprise than religious mission. It struggled to make a profit. The settlers found it difficult to provide for their basic needs, let alone turn their settlement into a profitable enterprise. They cast about for nearly a decade to find a suitable cash crop and finally found one in tobacco. The problem was that tobacco farming required many workers. As a result, the Virginia Company began to recruit indentured servants. These servants were willing to work in the colony in exchange for sea passage and a chance to become landowners, if

1. Nash, *Red, White, and Black*, 46.

they survived the hardships of their four-to-seven-year contracts. As the need for laborers increased, plantation owners turned from indentured British servants to African men and women enslaved in the Atlantic slave trade. In 1680, African people comprised about 7 percent of Virginia's population; by 1750, this number had risen to 44 percent, as servants declined and slaves increased.[2]

The first Africans who arrived in Jamestown in August 1619 were considered indentured servants and, like their British counterparts, could become landowners and marry when their indenture was completed. In 1621, one of these indentured Africans named Antonio, described simply as "a Negro," was sent to work on the Bennett plantation near the James River in Virginia. After completing his indenture and gaining his freedom, Antonio became the first African landowner in the Virginia colony. He changed his name to Anthony Johnson, married a Negro woman named Mary, and then moved his family to North Hampton County on Virginia's Eastern Shore, where he became prosperous enough to own livestock and five indentured servants. Eventually the Johnsons and their children moved to Maryland's Eastern Shore where they lived on their three-hundred-acre farm called "Tonies Vineyard." After her husband's death, Mary Johnson continued to manage the plantation, negotiating a ninety-nine-year lease, making a will, and leaving cattle to her grandchildren. She was the first and last Birthmother in the Chesapeake colonies to legally marry a free African man and live with her children on their own land.[3]

Although the Johnson family's success demonstrated that Africans could prosper in British colonial society, theirs was not the typical story. The Virginia planters needed a work force of dependable laborers, not a series of indentured servants who could earn freedom, property, and status. To that end, they developed a system of race-based slavery that eliminated legal marriage for the enslaved and made slavery a lifelong condition inherited through enslaved women.

In 1662, Virginia passed the Hereditary Slavery Law, which declared that "WHEREAS some doubts have arisen whether children got by any Englishman upon a negro woman should be slave or free, *Be it therefore enacted and declared by this present grand assembly*, that all children born in this country shall be held bond or free only according to the condition of

---

[2]. Kolchin, *American Slavery*, 11.

[3]. The story of Anthony and Mary Johnson follows the account in Breen and Innes, "Myne Owne Ground," 7–18.

the mother."[4] In other words, regardless of the father's race or legal status, a child born of a slave woman was considered a slave from birth, rather than inheriting rights from his or her father. In subsequent rulings, the rights of enslaved Africans were further restricted, and these laws were brought together and formalized in the Virginia Slave Codes of 1705.

What did the Hereditary Slavery Law and the Slave Codes mean for Birthmothers? They meant that Birthmothers could not legally marry. They could be traded at will, or even killed, by their owners. Their children, regardless of the father, were lifelong slaves. If the mother or the children ran away, they could be apprehended and prosecuted. They could not seek redress within the regular court system. They were officially considered "real estate." In every sense of the word, Birthmothers were now enslaved, without access to the kind of life that Mary Johnson had built for her family. Furthermore, these laws meant that Birthmothers were now central to the economic success of the colony.

The Virginia Slave Codes ensured that slave owners could realize perpetual profits from a slave labor force that reproduced itself from enslaved mothers and their children. These slaves became moveable property and capital that were more easily sold or traded than land. One slave owner calculated that his plantation made a 4 percent profit every year simply on the births of Black babies.[5] To reach this goal, a woman had to bear a child every two years. This made her more profitable than any man because she not merely worked, but also added to the capital assets of the plantation. Indeed, this owner told his manager that "with respect therefore to our women & their children I must pray you to inculcate upon [instruct] the overseers that it is not their labor, but their *increase* which is the first consideration with us" (authors' emphasis).[6] That is, perpetual pregnancy and childbirth, often brought about through routine sexual abuse, was not merely tolerated but promoted, since the birth of new slaves increased an owner's prosperity.

For a Birthmother, this use of her body was an evil beyond the toil and torture she shared with enslaved men and indentured white women. Her children, who did bring her some comfort, were not really hers, because they were under her owner's complete control. She and her children had no legitimacy. She had to struggle with owners for ways to raise her children

---

4. Hening, ed., *Statutes at Large*, 2:170 (modernized).
5. Wiencek, *Master of the Mountain*, 8–9.
6. Wiencek, *Master of the Mountain*, 250–51.

and direct their lives. Children of enslaved Birthmothers who were fathered by rich and famous white men were denied by their fathers and excluded by their white families. Indeed, the slave owner who calculated a 4 percent profit on Black babies and who turned pregnancy and childbirth into a commercial venture was none other than one of these rich and famous white men: Thomas Jefferson, the third president of the United States of America. Jefferson never publicly acknowledged his own complicity in the multiplication of slavery. But the multicolored faces of the Birthmothers' children and their family stories could not be silenced.

The Hemings Story Begins[7]

One of these family stories begins with a Birthmother whose name we do not know, but whose story was later told by her great-grandson, Madison Hemings. The story of this family has little to say directly about the Christian faith, but it is important because it illustrates the circumstances into which antebellum African American Christian women were born and the ways in which their lives, and the lives of their children, were forcibly constricted.

In an oral history recorded in 1873 when he was sixty-eight years old, Madison Hemings described his great-grandmother as a "full-blooded African woman" who was purchased by the Eppes family, early settlers in the Virginia colony. This slave woman lived near Williamsburg, a port city, and became pregnant by James Hemings, the captain of an English trading vessel. In 1735, she gave birth to a daughter, Elizabeth, while Captain Hemings was at sea. When he returned to Williamsburg and learned of his daughter's birth, James Hemings claimed Elizabeth, acknowledging her as his own flesh. Colonial law, however, did not recognize his claim. The child of an enslaved mother was herself a slave, the property of her mother's owners. The Eppeses refused to relinquish or even sell Elizabeth to her father. They brought both mother and daughter into the "great house" where they could keep an eye on them. Meanwhile, Captain Hemings continued to press his claim and even threatened to kidnap the child. Eventually, however, the captain sailed away from Williamsburg and did not return.

Elizabeth Hemings grew up as a mixed-race slave in the Eppes household, where her mother died. When she was eleven years old, one of the

---

7. The story of the Hemings family, on which the following sections are based, are recounted in Hemings, "Life Among the Lowly"; Gordon-Reed, *Hemingses of Monticello*; and Wiencek, *Master of the Mountain*.

Eppes's daughters, Martha, married John Wayles, a merchant who lived nearby. Elizabeth Hemings was then given to Martha Eppes Wayles as part of her inheritance. Martha gave birth to twins in 1746, both of whom died, and two years later to a daughter, also named Martha. Martha Eppes Wayles died shortly after her daughter's birth, leaving the thirteen-year-old Elizabeth as the primary nurse and surrogate mother for the infant Martha.

Despite this important responsibility, Elizabeth herself was not protected from sexual exploitation. At the age of eighteen, she gave birth to her first child, Mary, whose father was described by Madison Hemings as a "darker mulatto" but whose name and status of slave or free we do not know. As was true at her own birth, Elizabeth's new child belonged neither to her father nor to her mother, but was considered the property of the Wayles family. Elizabeth's next three children, probably fathered by the same man over the next six years, were equally enslaved: Martin, Betty Brown (her second name given possibly to distinguish her from her mother, who was also known as Betty), and Nancy. Elizabeth may also have given birth to another daughter, Dolly, between the births of Martin and Betty. Elizabeth Hemings was thus literally a slave Birthmother: she gave birth to the next generation of Wayles's slaves. But she also remained a surrogate mother to the motherless Martha Wayles. Martha's father named Elizabeth Hemings in his will as the property of his daughter, thus ensuring that Elizabeth would not come under the control of his two subsequent wives.

However, after the death of his third wife, Elizabeth Lomax Skelton, in 1761, John Wayles himself repossessed Elizabeth Hemings as his "concubine." She was twenty-six years old. In Virginia, a woman who lived with a man outside of marriage was legally defined as a concubine. For an enslaved woman, however, there was no choice in this matter of "living with a man." To be a concubine was to be forced to be a Birthmother to more slaves. John Wayles owned and controlled Elizabeth's body, and he owned and controlled their six children who were born in the following eleven years: Robert, James, Thenia, Critta, Peter, and Sally Hemings, who was born at Monticello after her father's death.

In 1772, the year before John Wayles died, his daughter Martha, now herself a young widow, married a nearby land owner, Thomas Jefferson. Martha brought a great deal of property to the marriage, including the Elk Hill Plantation, numerous field and artisan slaves, and, of course, her surrogate slave mother, Elizabeth Hemings. Several of Elizabeth's enslaved children also relocated to the new household at Monticello. These included

The Birthmothers

Martha Wayles Jefferson's own half-siblings. But even after she moved to Monticello, Elizabeth Hemings continued to enrich the Jefferson family by giving birth to at least two more children: John and Lucy. Their father was Jefferson's chief carpenter, Joseph Nielson. Nielson's apprentice William Fossett also apparently fathered Joseph, the son of Elizabeth's eldest daughter Mary. Although these two carpenters did not own Elizabeth and her daughter, the Hemings women were unprotected from the ever-present threat of rape that Birthmothers and their daughters could neither resist nor protest.

As an enslaved Birthmother, Elizabeth Hemings also had no control over her children's work or their futures. Their lives were now determined by their new owner. Elizabeth and her children were house slaves, who never worked in the plantation fields. They lived, along with other house slaves and skilled white artisans, in cabins scattered down the mountain from Monticello. By the end of his life, as one historian notes, "Jefferson looked down from his terrace onto a community of slaves he knew very well—an extended family and network of related families that had been in his ownership for two, three, or four generations.... They were all Hemingses by blood, descendants of the matriarch Elizabeth 'Betty' Hemings, or Hemings relatives by marriage."[8]

Jefferson made two of Elizabeth's sons his personal servants. Eighteen-year-old Martin Hemings became the butler at Monticello. Martha Jefferson's half-sibling Robert Hemings lived with Jefferson in Philadelphia when he wrote the Declaration of Independence as a member of the Continental Congress. Robert was then fourteen years old. Jefferson treated Elizabeth's other sons, however, like lower-class white men and placed them to work alongside skilled white artisans, implementing his blueprints and plans for buildings, gardens, factories, and mechanical devices at Monticello. Although Jefferson did not emancipate them, the Hemings men enjoyed some degree of freedom within the quasi-slave system he devised. For example, Elizabeth's son John had his own joinery, a shop that made cabinets, using the skills he had learned from his Irish father.

The grandchildren, however, did not fare as well. Several worked as "nail boys" in a factory that demanded a strict discipline. Boys as young as ten or twelve were required to show up for work before dawn at the nail forge down the mountain, even in icy midwinters. They were whipped to work efficiently, because profits from the factory paid the mansion's grocery

---

8. Wiencek, *Master of the Mountain*, 17.

bills. In one incident, Elizabeth's grandson James Hemings was whipped three times in one day by a factory manager when he was unable to work because of a fever. After recovering, he fled Monticello to join a community of free Black runaway slaves who were boatmen on the nearby James River. Although Jefferson tried unsuccessfully to convince him to return to Monticello, he stopped short of sending slave catchers to fetch the boy.[9]

Monticello, Jefferson's home in the sky, required a large number of slaves to work the plantations whose crops provided both food and income for the extended household. Although Jefferson helped to write the Declaration of Independence, slaves were not included among the colonists who sought freedom. Jefferson, along with many other white landowners, was unwilling to give up his dependence on slaves for his family's emotional, financial, and physical security. Yet some enslaved people reached out for that freedom. During the Revolutionary War, one Birthmother, "Black Sal," learned that Lord Dunmore, leader of the British forces, had promised freedom for slaves who left their masters and reached the British lines. She managed to escape from Jefferson's Elk Hill plantation with her three children and reach the British encampment. But Sal's two daughters soon died from smallpox, and she returned to the plantation with her son. Jefferson noted the deaths of young Flora (age eight) and Quomina (age six) as a simple loss of property, writing in his farm book: "joined enemy and died."[10]

Although Elizabeth Hemings and her daughters did not work in the fields, as Sal and her children were forced to do, they remained slaves at the "big house," supporting Thomas Jefferson and his wife, Martha Wayles Jefferson. Indeed, from birth Martha Jefferson had looked to Elizabeth Hemings as her surrogate mother and depended upon her. Only nine months after her own marriage to Jefferson, Martha gave birth to a daughter, also named Martha, but usually called "Patsy." Because Martha had difficulty nursing the baby, a slave woman named Ursula Granger, who had recently birthed a son Archy, was assigned to nurse the infant Martha. Over the next ten years, Martha Jefferson became pregnant at least five more times, her health worsening with each miscarriage and birth. In May 1782, her last child, Lucy Elizabeth, was born, named after a sibling who had died the previous year. Martha Jefferson did not long survive this birth. As she lay dying, she was surrounded by her young daughters, Jefferson's sisters, her surrogate mother, and her own enslaved siblings, the daughters of

---

9. Wiencek, *Master of the Mountain*, 122–23.
10. Wiencek, *Master of the Mountain*, 63–64.

Elizabeth Hemings. Thomas Jefferson was also present, and Martha made him solemnly promise that he would never marry again, a promise that he kept. She died with the assurance that if Jefferson remained unmarried, her children would be cared for by her surrogate mother, Elizabeth Hemings, and by her own half-siblings, Elizabeth's daughters.

Sally Hemings in Paris

Two years later in 1784, in spite of his reluctance to leave Monticello, Jefferson accepted an assignment by the Continental Congress to go to Paris to participate in negotiations for peace with Great Britain on behalf of the new nation. He left his youngest daughters, Mary (also known as Polly) and Lucy Elizabeth with their aunt Elizabeth Eppes, younger sister of his deceased wife. He also left eleven-year-old Sally Hemings, daughter of Elizabeth Hemings and herself a half-sibling of their deceased mother and thus a half-aunt to the two young girls, to help care for Polly and Lucy. He decided to take his eldest daughter Patsy, now age twelve, along with Elizabeth Hemings's nineteen-year-old son James, to Paris with him.

The Jefferson party arrived in France in August 1784, where they would remain for the next five years. Patsy was placed in a convent's boarding school for girls, James began training to become a French chef, and Jefferson moved into Hôtel de Langeac, which became his Parisian residence. When Jefferson learned that his two-year-old daughter Lucy had died in Virginia, he sent for nine-year-old Polly to join him in France, accompanied by a married slave woman named Isabel Hern. Isabel was unable to make the journey, so Polly's young aunt Sally Hemings, whom she had known all her life, became her companion. Polly and Sally undertook a five-week sea voyage to London, where they stayed for three weeks with Abigail and John Adams. They eventually joined Patsy, Jefferson, and James Hemings in Paris.

When Polly was sent to the convent school with her sister Patsy, the Hemings siblings found themselves with considerable free time. They moved through the city along with the hundreds of free people of color who lived there. Unlike Monticello, a rural colonial plantation estate dominated and controlled by Jefferson, the Hemingses were now living in cosmopolitan Paris, the largest city in Europe. They resided near neighborhoods with large numbers of Black people from French colonies and had contact with fellow servants, both Black and white, in their residence and in other households. James Heming received a wage of $4.00 a month for his work as a chef in the Jefferson household, and Sally received an intermittent salary for her house work.

In fact, although Jefferson remained their owner, the Hemings siblings were legally free. Louis X in the fourteenth century had articulated the "Freedom Principle," which held that "every slave who stepped onto French soil was free." Jefferson, in fact, was obligated by law to register the Hemings siblings as slaves, although he failed to do so, and both James and Sally could have sued for their freedom in the French courts. The Parisian Admiralty Court routinely granted freedom to every petitioner who applied, nearly two hundred by the end of the eighteenth century. The Hemingses, however, did not formally respond to this promise of freedom, but continued to live under Jefferson's direction.[11]

James was kept busy pursuing his trade as a chef and learning to speak French. Sally had fewer responsibilities since the Jefferson girls were away at school. Heavy cleaning and other chores were performed by the French servants at the residence, but Sally was occasionally expected to help her brother prepare and serve large meals. She served as a lady's maid to Patsy and Polly when they were home from school. Sally also began to do the sewing and mending for the family, skills that were expected of all women of the time, regardless of rank. When she returned to Monticello, she continued to serve as the principal seamstress, efficiently managing Jefferson's wardrobe.

In Paris, however, this intimate domestic duty brought her into close daily contact with Jefferson in his private quarters. She was a young, lone, unsupervised female without the scrutiny and buffer that might be provided by the presence of other women in the household. Although rapes occurred on plantations like Monticello, there was also a community of enslaved women to both warn of the danger and offer support to young women who were in vulnerable situations. We do not know when Jefferson began sexual relations with the teenage Sally. But the contact between the middle-aged widower and his enslaved adolescent girl, who was said to resemble his former wife, led to an expected outcome. Madison Hemings simply records that "During that time my mother became Mr. Jefferson's concubine."[12] We do know that during the final months in Paris, Sally became pregnant and that she remained Jefferson's enslaved mistress for the rest of her life.

11. Gordon-Reed, *Hemingses*, 175–76.
12. Hemings, "Life Among the Lowly."

The Birthmothers

The pregnancy raised a moral and ethical issue for James and Sally Hemings. Jefferson expected them to return with him to Virginia, but they now had other options. They could remain in Paris, free to work and support themselves as did other servants of color in the city. James could work as a chef and Sally as a chamber maid. The pregnancy, however, meant that they also needed to consider the fate of a third person. To stay in Paris meant freedom for themselves and for Sally's unborn child. But it also meant a permanent estrangement from their family, and it appears that Sally was homesick for her mother and sisters and craved their support. However, this sixteen-year-old concubine stood up to the influential Jefferson. As Madison Hemings recalls,

> He desired to bring my mother back to Virginia with him but she demurred. She was just beginning to understand the French language well, and in France she was free, while if she returned to Virginia she would be re-enslaved. So she refused to return with him. To induce her to do so he promised her extraordinary privileges, and made a solemn pledge that her children should be freed at the age of twenty-one years.[13]

Jefferson had much to lose: not just the prospect of domestic companionship and comfort, but also his reputation as a pro-liberty and anti-slavery advocate. If Sally Hemings had gone to the Admiralty Court to sue for her freedom, Jefferson's role as a slave owner would have been publicly exposed. As one historian has noted, "To have Jefferson, of all people, act in direct opposition to France's Freedom Principle so he could keep control over a sixteen-year-old enslaved girl would have been a spectacle for the ages."[14] Jefferson therefore promised Sally "extraordinary privileges" and made a solemn pledge to free her children at age twenty-one. Madison Hemings adds, "In consequence of his promises, on which she implicitly relied, [Sally] returned with him to Virginia."[15] The power she had held in France as a free woman disappeared.

Thomas Jefferson, his daughters, and the Hemings siblings left Paris in September 1789. After stopping in Norfolk in November, the party arrived at Monticello that December, where they were welcomed by their matriarch, Birthmother Elizabeth Hemings, now in her mid-fifties. There is little evidence that Elizabeth Hemings knew much about her teenage children's lives

---

13. Hemings, "Life Among the Lowly."
14. Gordon-Reed, *Hemingses*, 347.
15. Hemings, "Life Among the Lowly."

while they were living abroad, and she certainly had no control over their circumstances. Both had been taken to France without her consent or even input. While they were away, she lived at Tufton, one of Jefferson's farms, perhaps in semi-retirement. But she returned to Monticello in 1790 when seventeen-year-old Sally gave birth to a child who died shortly thereafter.

Soon after his own return, Jefferson visited the store of Colonel Thomas Bell in Charlottesville because he learned that in his absence, Mary Hemings, Elizabeth's oldest daughter, had hired herself out as a housekeeper to Bell.[16] "Hiring out" or working for another slave owner was an arrangement between slave owners that allowed the enslaved to change owners and improve their situation. Mary Hemings left Monticello, accompanied by two of her children, Joseph and Betsy, both probably fathered by William Fossett, and moved in with Bell, with whom she had two more children. Jefferson, however, still legally owned Mary and all her children. In fact, he gave her two older children, Daniel Farley and Molly Hemings, as wedding presents when they were still young teenagers. In the course of negotiations with Jefferson, Bell agreed to buy Mary and their two children, but Jefferson took the Fossett-Hemings children back to Monticello. Twelve-year-old Joseph was sent to work in the nailery and nine-year-old Betsy began work as a house girl in the mansion.

Shortly after they returned from Paris, Martha "Patsy" Jefferson became engaged to her cousin Thomas Mann Randolph. Jefferson drew up a marriage settlement that gave her twenty-seven slaves, her half-cousin Molly Hemings, and part of an outlying plantation. He did not, however, give her Sally, who remained at Monticello as Jefferson's concubine.

As Jefferson pursued his political ambitions, first as secretary of state, then as vice president, and finally as president, he continued to expand his family at Monticello. Shortly before taking office as vice president in 1797, he learned of the death of his and Sally's second child, two-year-old Harriet. When Jefferson came home the next summer, his first son to live to adulthood, William Beverly, was born. After the death of another infant daughter, a second baby Harriet was born in 1801. During Jefferson's two terms as president, Sally gave birth to two more sons: Madison in 1805 and Eston in 1808. In all, Sally Hemings had at least seven pregnancies in the years that she lived as Jefferson's concubine. Madison described a relatively happy childhood: the children "were always permitted to be with our mother, who was well used. It was her duty, all her life which I can remember, up to the

---

16. Gordon-Reed, *Hemingses*, 572.

time of father's death, to take care of his chamber and wardrobe, look after us children and do such light work as sewing." He also remembered, however, that his father "was not in the habit of showing partiality or fatherly affection to us children."[17] When he was fourteen, Madison was put into the carpenter's trade under his Uncle John.

No matter how idyllic and loving Madison's childhood, scandal and rumor shadowed Jefferson and Sally's relationship. Jefferson's white family and defenders claimed that Sally's children were fathered by a relative, while his political opponents criticized him for the affair. Jefferson himself remained silent, neither defending nor confirming his relationship with Sally Hemings. In the twentieth century, DNA evidence confirmed Jefferson's paternity, but historians, reporters, and the general public have been slow to recognize the importance of the Hemings family to Jefferson's life and fortune. Guests to Monticello who admire its beauty and organization have attributed the mansion and its grounds primarily to Jefferson's genius, rather than crediting the skill and efficiency of Elizabeth Hemings, her sons, her daughters, and her grandchildren who helped to build and sustain the industrious, well-organized enterprise.

The Hemings Legacy

During the lifetime of Elizabeth Hemings, a revolution had made Jefferson the president of the United States, and a religious awakening, which we will consider in the next chapter, led to the conversion of many African Americans to Christianity. However, neither revolution nor revival freed Elizabeth Hemings and her children from the inhumane system that controlled their lives from birth to death.

In 1807 when Elizabeth Hemings died, eight of her known twelve children were still alive, along with over thirty grandchildren and at least four great grandchildren.[18] She had not been worked to death by slavery, but she was held in bondage by the perpetual mothering that increased the wealth of the men who owned her. Jefferson's calculation that his plantation made a 4 percent profit every year on the births of Black babies was realized through the bodies of Elizabeth Hemings and her daughters. As Elizabeth Hemings lay dying, her three-year-old grandson Madison sat in the house, eating some bread. He offered his grandmother a piece, but she

17. Hemings, "Life Among the Lowly."
18. Gordon-Reed, *Hemingses*, 586.

Faith Confronts Evil

declined: "Granny don't want bread any more."[19] Shortly thereafter she died and found freedom at last.

Although the Hemingses were favored slaves of Jefferson, they were still slaves. Jefferson sold two of Elizabeth's older children to a nearby plantation owner and gave a grandchild as a wedding present to his own daughter. Two other sons, however, were formally emancipated by Jefferson, and their skills and talents provided some measure of security. Mary Hemings Bell was allowed to live in her own house in Charlottesville. Jefferson also privately freed Harriet and William Beverly and helped them leave Monticello and pass into the white world. Sally, however, along with her sons Madison and Eston, remained enslaved.

It was not until 1826, just before his death, that Jefferson freed Madison and his brother Eston, finally fulfilling the promise he had made thirty-seven years earlier to Sally Hemings in Paris. He prepared a document that stated "I give also to John Hemings the service of his two apprentices, Madison and Eston Hemings, until their respective ages of twenty-one years, at which period, respectively, I give them their freedom; and I humbly and earnestly request of the Legislature of Virginia a confirmation of the bequest of freedom to these servants, with permission to remain in this State, where their families and connections are."[20] This emancipation of his sons was couched in complex legal language that attempted to conceal his paternal connection to the young men. It suggested that his generosity was primarily directed toward his valued servant John Hemings, not to his own children. In fact, at the time of this emancipation document, Madison was already twenty-one. Once freed, Madison and Eston rented a house in Charlottesville. Madison married, and when Sally Hemings was given her "time" and released from service, she moved in with Madison and his wife. After her death, Madison with his wife and daughter moved to Ohio, a free state, where he worked as a carpenter.

Sally Hemings's legacy to her children and grandchildren was freedom. Although she birthed her children into slavery and remained enslaved to Jefferson as long as he lived, all four of her surviving children lived out their days as free men and women, although they were not able to claim Jefferson's name or wealth.

Jefferson's other slaves were not as fortunate. His white family separated and sold slave families to settle his speculations and debts after his death.

---

19. Hemings, "Life Among the Lowly."
20. Gordon-Reed, *Hemingses*, 648.

The Birthmothers

The January 1827 auction, which included the contents of Monticello and at least 130 "valuable negros," reveals the cruel economics of slavery. One family was divided among eight different buyers and another set among seven individual buyers. Nine-year-old Caroline Hughes, the daughter of Jefferson's gardener Wormley Hughes and a great-granddaughter of Elizabeth Hemings, was sold separate from her family.

The Fossett family was also split up. Although Jefferson's will freed Mary Hemings's son Joseph Fossett, his wife Edith, who had been Jefferson's cook, and their children were left enslaved. His eldest child already had been given to Jefferson's own grandson. At the auction, which Joseph Fossett attended, his brother-in-law Jesse Scott purchased Edith and the two youngest children, William and Daniel, to keep them safe. But eleven-year-old Peter was forced to stand alone on the auction block. The three daughters, Maria, Patsy, and Isabella were sold to three different buyers, although Patsy soon escaped from her new owner. Nothing is known of her life after this event. Joseph Fossett spent the next ten years working to earn enough money to buy back his family. Scott relinquished Edith, William, and Daniel, but Peter's owner, John R. Jones, refused to close a negotiated deal. Eventually, Joseph and his wife left Charlottesville for Ohio, leaving most of their family behind.[21]

Peter Fossett, however, persevered, teaching other slaves to read and write, forging emancipation documents for himself and others, running away, and standing once again on an auction block in Charlottesville after his second escape attempt. But as he testified later in life, "God raised up friends for me."[22] These friends purchased his freedom and sent him to Ohio where he served as a Baptist minister and with the Underground Railroad.

The auction of the families at Monticello laid bare the suffering caused by slavery's generational evil that was legally passed from Birthmothers to their children. The Birthmothers created families, but they were also forced to create property. Human slaves were reduced to capital that subsidized the white families and kept them from financial disaster and catastrophe. Elizabeth Hemings and her daughters were able to ensure some benefits for their children. But they were unable to control their destinies, which remained firmly within the hands of the white owners. Even emancipation, which Jefferson had promised to Sally's children, remained his choice to the end.

21. Gordon-Reed, *Hemingses*, 655–56; Wiencek, *Master of the Mountain*, 3–4, 263.
22. Wiencek, *Master of the Mountain*, 4.

The Legacy of the Birthmothers

The history of African American Christian women begins with Birthmothers who were the hopeful survivors of an evil beyond toil and torture. For the sake of their children, these Birthmothers chose to live. They summoned the physical strength to birth, rather than to abort or kill, the children conceived by rape. Some, like Sally Hemings, chose to leave the promise of freedom for themselves in order to ensure it for their children. Not all Birthmothers shared Sally Hemings's unique and privileged position, but others made difficult choices to remain in their children's lives in any way possible, including continued submission to their owners. The survival of enslaved children depended on Birthmothers who chose to nurture and feed them with the love, food, and hope needed for their humanity and survival. Birthmothers chose to work around or in opposition to their owners' purposes. With help from other enslaved women, they began their own families. Although most Birthmothers served and suffered under their owners, others, like Black Sal, chose to escape and risk themselves and their children to be free. Some Birthmothers were also among the first African Americans to choose to become Christians.

There is little evidence that either Elizabeth or Sally Hemings were touched by the religious revivals that swept through the United States in the eighteenth and nineteenth centuries. We know nothing of their adherence, or nonadherence, to Christianity. Jefferson himself was indifferent to orthodox Christianity, and this may have contributed to his reluctance to emancipate his slaves. One historian has astutely noted that Virginia slave owners who did free their slaves were "strongly influenced" by their religious faith, but that "Jefferson, a creature of ethics, was not like them. . . . The ethical sense has never been so good at exciting passionate, caution-thrown-to-the-wind actions" such as would be required to give up property and prosperity. She concludes, "Jefferson opted for a different course: one that allowed him to continue to espouse the progressive belief in emancipation, thus holding on to his very deep need to be seen as an intelligent man of the future, while maintaining the lifestyle to which he had become accustomed."[23]

Other slaves at Monticello, however, were strengthened in their difficult lives by their faith. One such Birthmother, Hannah, was born at Monticello but later served as a cook at Jefferson's country retreat, ninety miles

---

23. Gordon-Reed, *Hemingses*, 112.

away. On November 15, 1818, when Jefferson was in his late seventies, Hannah wrote him a prayerful message, which has been preserved among his papers:

> Master, I write you a few lines to let you know that your house and furniture are all safe, as I expect you will be glad to know. . . . I was sorry to hear that you was so unwell you could not come [here]. It grieve me many time, but I hope as you have been so blessed in this [life] that you considered it was God that done it and no other one. We all ought to be thankful for what he has done for us, we ought to serve and obey his commandments that you may set to win the prize and after glory, run.
>
> Master I do not [think] my ignorant letter will be much encouragement to you as knows I am a poor, ignorant creature.
>
> Adieu, I am your humble servant Hannah.[24]

Although this letter is written within the protocols and humility of slave culture, it also transcends them. Jefferson did not encourage literacy or Christian faith among his slaves, but Hannah's letter stands as a powerful counterweight to these prohibitions. Furthermore, she not only encouraged her master, but she also exhorted him to thank and serve God, paraphrasing the words of Saint Paul in 1 Corinthians 9:24: "Know ye not that they which run in a race run all, but one receiveth the prize? So run, that ye may obtain" (KJV). Her paraphrase used the words of the hymn "Evening Shade": "May we set out to win the prize / And after glory run." Hannah probably learned both Scripture and the hymn by attending the African meeting house near the plantation where she was enslaved. Her faith and her literacy empowered her to speak boldly and directly to Jefferson. She embodied the next generations of African Americans, awakened by conversion to Christ, who would build upon the Birthmothers' choices for their survival.

---

24. Quoted in Wiencek, *Master of the Mountain*, 127 (modernized).

2

The Road to Conversion

I want Jesus to walk with me.
All along my pilgrim journey,
Lord, I want Jesus to walk with me.

—A̲FRICAN A̲MERICAN S̲PIRITUAL

A SPIRITUAL REVIVAL OCCURRED around Elizabeth Hemings and her family, although it seems not to have touched them directly. This revival transformed the lives of imported and native-born enslaved Africans as many converted to Christianity. The road to their conversion meant accepting the religion of those who caused their suffering, doubted their humanity, and wavered about baptizing or worshipping with them in their churches. Although some may have been introduced to Christianity by Catholic merchants and missionaries in Africa, the first Christians most enslaved Africans in the British colonies encountered were slave traders and seamen on slave ships. It was not an auspicious beginning.[1]

---

1. Chapter 2 draws on the work of Raboteau, *Slave Religion*; and Creel, "Peculiar People."

Resistance to Conversion

After their arrival in North America, the enslaved were bought by, and lived and worked on the same land as, Christian settlers, overseers, and indentured servants. They shared natural disasters, plagues, and wars. Yet they remained two distinct groups—free and unfree—with little knowledge about their different beliefs and cultures.

The white Christians were members of various Protestant denominations scattered across the thirteen colonies: Puritans in New England; Episcopalians or Church of England in the southern colonies; Dutch Reformed in New York; Lutherans in New Jersey; and Baptists, Methodists, and Presbyterians in the mid-Atlantic colonies. The enslaved Africans came from nearly one hundred different African nations and societies. They included Yorubas, Fulanis, and Igbos from West Africa, and the Akan and Bantu speakers from Congo-Angola. In spite of this diversity, white owners and settlers subscribed to a view of Africans stated in 1450 by the Portuguese writer Gomes Eannes de Azurara. He argued that all Africans "lived in perdition of soul and body; of their souls, in that they were yet pagans, without the clearness and the light of the holy faith; and of their bodies, in that they lived like beasts, without any custom of reasonable beings."[2] Like Azurara, many settlers believed slavery was justified because it was a way to spread the gospel to uncivilized Africans.

Although some clergy were quietly angered by the brutal treatment of the enslaved, most Christian settlers accepted slavery. There was little moral debate or outrage at its impact on tortured Africans because white Christians were convinced that the sin of blackness, which cursed the African, outweighed the sins of slavery. In spite of these beliefs about the enslaved Africans, the English king Charles II urged the Council for Foreign Plantations in 1660

> to consider how such of the Natives or such as are purchased by you from other parts to be servants or slaves may best be invited to the Christian Faith, and be made capable of being baptized thereunto, it being to the honor of our Crown and of the Protestant Religion that all persons in any of our Dominions should be taught the knowledge of God, and be made acquainted with the mysteries of Salvation.[3]

---

2. Quoted in Raboteau, *Slave Religion*, 97.
3. Quoted in Raboteau, *Slave Religion*, 97 (modernized).

The Road to Conversion

Colonial governors were instructed to assist the conversion of "Negroes and Indians" to Christianity. However, some colonists believed Africans were another species who should not receive the Christian sacraments of baptism and the Lord's Supper. A French Anglican missionary in 1709 objected that "Many Masters can't be persuaded that Negroes and Indians are otherwise than Beasts."[4] Forty years later, a Swedish visitor complained that "the masters of these negroes in most of the English colonies take little care of their spiritual welfare."[5]

Owners also resisted converting the enslaved because they feared baptism would force them to emancipate their Christian slaves. Baptism, which meant inclusion in the body of Christ, suggested human equality along the lines of Galatians 3:28: "There is neither Jew nor Greek, there is neither bond nor free, there is neither male nor female: for ye are all one in Christ Jesus" (KJV). To resolve debates about the impact of baptism on the slaves' status, six colonial legislatures passed acts asserting that baptism did not alter a slave's condition. If enslaved before baptism, she or he remained enslaved after baptism.

A Virginia act passed in 1667 stated explicitly that

> Whereas some doubts have arisen whether children that are slaves by birth, and by the charity and pity of their owners made partakers of the blessed sacrament of baptism, should by virtue of their baptism be made free, it is enacted that *baptism does not alter the condition of the person as to his bondage or freedom; masters freed from this doubt may more carefully propagate Christianity by permitting slaves to be admitted to that sacrament.*[6]

Mandatory church attendance in observance of the Sabbath was another obstacle to converting the enslaved. Christian owners, who were themselves forbidden to work on the Sabbath, often forced their enslaved Africans to work at their accustomed tasks. Other plantation owners set aside Sundays for the enslaved to tend to the plots allotted for growing food for themselves and their families.

With Sundays often unavailable, clergy found it difficult to find times when slaves could be instructed. Even when allowed to do so, the scarcity of clergy in the colonies presented an additional obstacle. One study reported that half of the Church of England parishes in Virginia were without clergy.

---

4. Quoted in Raboteau, *Slave Religion*, 100–101.
5. Quoted in Raboteau, *Slave Religion*, 102.
6. Higginbotham Jr., *In the Matter of Color*, 36–37.

Georgia boasted only two churches at a distance of 150 miles from each other. South Carolina had only a single church in Charleston. To augment the lack of regular clergy, the missionary arm of the Church of England, The Society for the Propagation of the Gospel in Foreign Parts (SPG), was organized in 1701. Its particular focus was sending missionaries to British colonies around the world.[7]

SPG missionaries and regular clergy alike were often overwhelmed, however, by linguistic and literacy obstacles. Africans who arrived on the slave ships barely spoke or understood English. They were also unfamiliar with the Christian narrative in the Bible, a written text that they could not read. Some colonial religious leaders insisted these difficulties were racial and insurmountable. In 1699, the Virginia House of Burgesses stated that

> the negroes born in this country are generally baptised and brought up in the Christian religion; but for negroes imported hither, the gross bestiality and rudeness of their manners, the variety and strangeness of their languages, and the weakness and shallowness of their minds, render it in a manner impossible to make any progress in their conversion.[8]

White Christians failed to recognize that the enslaved were a displaced and traumatized people. Africans were being forced to make sense of the precepts and practices of a new culture and language and religion while trying at the same time to survive the harsh brutality of slavery.

Some enslaved Africans deliberately rejected Christian conversion because they were determined to remember and retain the customs and language of their own people and societies. Leonard Haynes recalled that his grandfather had been an African priest before being sold to a plantation owner in Georgia. As a priest, he remained hostile to Christianity throughout his life.[9] On large plantations and farms, hidden from their owners and other white people, enslaved groups secretly practiced indigenous African religious rites. A few Muslims continued their prayer rituals. Although Omar Ibn Said, a slave in North Carolina, later converted to Christianity, he wrote his memoir in Arabic script and stated without regret that "Before I came to the Christian country, my religion was the religion of Mohammed."[10] Other enslaved persons who practiced Islam in Africa

7. Raboteau, *Slave Religion*, 104–5.
8. Quoted in Raboteau, *Slave Religion*, 100.
9. Raboteau, *Slave Religion*, 46.
10. Quoted in Raboteau, *Slave Religion*, 46.

combined their ancestral faith with Christianity, recognizing Allah as the God of both religions.

The clergy and missionaries seemed oblivious that obstacles to African conversion could include displacement and trauma, as well as intentional cultural resistance by the enslaved who were trying to retain and choose their own religious practices and beliefs. Instead, the frustrated evangelists attributed the enslaved people's slow response to conversion to the African's childlike nature. They turned to catechistic regiments and rote memorization designed for children to make the enslaved recite Scripture and prayers in order to show their readiness for conversion. Some owners forced their slaves to attend church services with them, but seated in separate areas, where they could hear sermons from preachers. One such preacher, Rev. Thomas Bacon, told his enslaved congregants:

> And pray, do not think that I want to deceive you, when I tell you that your *masters* and *mistresses* are God's *overseers,*—and that if you are faulty towards them, God himself will punish you severely for it in the next world, unless you repent of it and strive to make amends by your *faithfulness* and *Diligence*.[11]

Such sermons offered little hope for the enslaved and did not encourage true conversion.

Beginning the Road to Conversion

Some clergy focused less on the enslaved resistance to conversion and their need for obedience to owners than on the owners' own need to behave as true Christians. The Puritan preacher Cotton Mather published *The Negro Christianized* in 1706. While this religious tract approved of slavery as an institution, it did call on white owners to earnestly instruct their "servants" in the Christian faith. It was their duty to attend to the spiritual needs of everyone in their household. This included Africans who were rational human beings, not beasts of burden: "Show yourselves men," he argued, "and let rational arguments have their force upon you, to make you treat, not as brutes but as men, those rational creatures whom God has made your servants."[12] Mather continued: "Thou shalt love thy neighbor as thyself. Man, thy Negro is thy neighbor. T'were an ignorance, unworthy of a man,

---

11. Higginbotham Jr., *In the Matter of Color*, 37.
12. Mather, *Negro Christianized*, 3 (modernized).

to imagine otherwise. Yea, if thou dost grant, that God hath made of one blood all nations of men [Acts 17:26, KJV], he is thy brother too."[13]

Later in this tract, Mather further argued that God did not distinguish among people on the basis of their race or color:

> Their complexion sometimes is made an argument, why nothing should be done for them.... As if the great God went by the complexion of men, in his favors to them! As if none but Whites might hope to be favored and accepted with God! ... Away with such trifles! The God who looks on the heart is not moved by the color of the skin; is not more propitious to one color than another. Say rather, with the Apostle (Acts 10:34, 35), "Of a truth I perceive, that God is no respecter of persons; but in every nation, he that feareth him and worketh righteousness is accepted with him."[14]

Despite Mather's theological arguments that enslaved Africans were human beings, brothers, and loved by God, he did not argue that the institution of slavery itself was wrong. The Society of Negroes that he organized met every Sunday evening, but the enslaved who gathered were simply taught to sing hymns and recite the catechism that Mather had published in *The Negro Christianized*. They remained slaves.

Nevertheless, a growing body of enslaved Christians was emerging, and women were at the forefront on this road to conversion. We do not know many of their names, but we do know some. The first recorded baptisms of enslaved Africans were those of Anthony, Isabel, and their son William on February 16, 1623 in Elizabeth City County, Virginia.[15] The first enslaved person to be baptized in New England, of which we have a written record, was a woman in Dorchester, Massachusetts who belonged to Rev. Stoughton and was recognized for her "sound knowledge and true godliness."[16]

Nearly a century later, the poet Lucy Terry Prince, whose orally preserved poem is the earliest known work of literature by an African American, was baptized at age five into the First Church of Deerfield (Massachusetts) in 1735. When she died in 1821, her obituary, printed in both *The Vermont Gazette* and *The Franklin Herald* (Massachusetts), noted that "she was early devoted to God in Baptism." It recorded that she joined the church as an adult at age fourteen. In paying tribute to this "remarkable

---

13. Mather, *Negro Christianized*, 4 (modernized).
14. Mather, *Negro Christianized*, 15 (modernized).
15. Mitchell, *Black Preaching*, 23.
16. Raboteau, *Slave Religion*, 109.

woman," the obituary concluded that "she was much respected among her acquaintance, who treated her with a degree of deference."[17]

These recorded baptisms were only a few of those that brought enslaved persons into the Christian church. Evangelizing, conversion, and baptism of the enslaved continued through the New England and southern colonies, but numbers were relatively small. The first enslaved African converts received into the Church of England at Goose Creek, South Carolina, were taught and baptized by Rev. Samuel Thomas in the late 1600s.[18] SPG missionary Francis Le Jau, who followed Thomas at Goose Creek, wrote letters documenting the abuse suffered by the enslaved, but he also required each one to vow, before receiving baptism, that she or he did not "ask for the holy baptism out of any design to free yourself from the Duty and Obedience that you owe to your Master while you live, but merely for the good of Your Soul."[19] Le Jau insisted on extensive instruction, including teaching the enslaved to read. He devised careful methods to evangelize both Africans and Indians, meeting them after church and teaching them the Apostle's Creed, the Lord's Prayer, the Ten Commandments, and some portion of the catechism. These methods demanded time and energy that many, both enslaved and owners, were unable or unwilling to invest. Clergy and missionaries in both the North and the South documented the individuals and small groups of African converts they successfully instructed. But most enslaved Africans, like most white servants in the colonies, remained unconverted and unchurched. This was largely because they lacked the language and literacy skills required as evidence of conversion.

Something more than knowledge and recitation of biblical and theological texts was needed to meet the spiritual needs of hardworking white servants and enslaved Africans. Before the Great Awakening revivals of the mid-1700s, evangelizing and conversion in the colonies remained stymied by the same issues faced by the apostle Paul in building the earliest churches: "How then shall they call on him in whom they have not believed? and how shall they believe in him of whom they have not heard? and how shall they hear without a preacher?" (Rom 10:14, KJV).

---

17. Quoted in Proper, "Lucy Terry Prince," 188.
18. Raboteau, *Slave Religion*, 115–16.
19. Quoted in Raboteau, *Slave Religion*, 123.

The Great Awakenings

Conversions and religious activities in the colonies greatly increased with the arrival of George Whitefield, a master of open-air preaching and a stirring orator and spokesperson for "vital religion and justification by faith." Whitefield was part of the Methodist missionary movement in England led by Charles and John Wesley along with a group of Anglican believers at Oxford University. This movement met the religious needs of the poor classes in London with an evangelical style of worship and distinctive "methods" (hence, Methodism). These methods included organizing new converts into societies under lay leaders and itinerant pastors. The Great Awakening revival had its "first stirrings" in 1734 among both Black and white congregants at Puritan Jonathan Edward's church in Northampton, Massachusetts. But it struck with full force when Whitefield began his second preaching tour in the United States in 1740.

Whitefield's preaching pushed aside the instructional approaches to conversion favored by the colonial clergy and missionaries. Like them, his authority was the Bible, but Whitefield preached extemporaneously on Jesus as savior and deliverance from sin. His stress on "glad tidings," inner change, and the experience of conversion, rather than on instruction and recitation, made Christianity more appealing and accessible to a wider public. Whitefield held interracial revival meetings. He appeared in Middleton, Connecticut before four thousand listeners in one of the largest public gatherings held before the American Revolution.

His preaching attracted both enslaved and free Africans like Olaudah Equiano, who witnessed him preach at a church service in Philadelphia. Equiano was baptized as Gustavus Vassa in the Anglican Church after being kidnapped as a child from Benin, West Africa. He was brought as a slave to Montserrat and the southern colonies in North America. Of his encounter with Whitefield, Equiano wrote, "When I got into the church I saw this pious man exhorting the people with the greatest fervour and earnestness, and sweating as much as I ever did while in slavery at Montserrat beach. I was very much struck and impressed with this; I thought it strange I had never seen divines [preachers] exert themselves in this manner before, and was no longer at a loss to account for the thin congregations they preached to."[20] Equiano warmed to this presentation of the gospel. As one historian of African American Christianity has noted, Whitefield "built the bridge

---

20. Equiano, *Interesting Narrative*, 184.

The Road to Conversion

over which [Protestant Christianity] could travel to a spiritually hungry and brutally oppressed people from Africa."[21]

As the Great Awakening revival spread, it encouraged ordinary women and men, including white servants and enslaved Africans, to testify about their conversions. Such lay exhorting was not favored by the established clergy. They thought it encouraged social leveling, pushed aside denominational differences, and opened church roles that should be reserved for educated religious leaders. But those who had been revived and awakened disagreed. They laid hold of grace through conversions based on inner change rather than through intellectual assent. And they testified to their conversions. But at the same time, the Great Awakening also pushed forward the importance of literacy for the enslaved.

In 1739 while in North Carolina, Whitefield described his visit with an enslaved family belonging to his host. After visiting a sick man and praying with his children, Whitefield wrote, "This more and more convinces me that Negro children if early brought up in the nurture and admonition of the Lord would make as great proficiency as many white children." He then vowed, "I do not despair, if God spares my life, of seeing a school of young Negroes singing the praises of Him Who made them in a psalm of thanksgiving. Lord, Thou has put into my heart a good design to educate them."[22]

A year later, Whitefield traveled from Philadelphia to Savannah on horseback, preaching as he went. He continued to observe the pervasive institution of slavery. During his journey, Whitefield insisted to his plantation hosts that he be allowed to discuss the doctrines of free grace and salvation with the enslaved. He demanded that he be allowed to explain that the enslaved could also attain this new birth. Both women and men responded to his teaching. We have a vivid first-person account from one young man who was "awakened" during a service in Charleston, South Carolina.

John Marrant, a literate freeborn African American musician, was a wild young teenager. He described himself as "unstable as water."[23] One evening, he accepted a dare to crash a meeting where "a crazy man was hallooing" and to cause a disturbance by playing his French horn.[24] What happened next changed his life:

---

21. Mitchell, *Black Preaching*, 34.
22. Quoted in Creel, "*Peculiar People,*" 86 (modernized).
23. Marrant, *Narrative*, 9.
24. Marrant, *Narrative*, 10.

> I was pushing the people to make room, to get the horn off my shoulder to blow it, just as Mr. Whitefield was naming his text, and looking round, and, as I thought, directly upon me and pointing with his finger, he uttered these words, "Prepare to meet thy God, O Israel." The Lord accompanied the word with such power, that I was struck to the ground, and lay both speechless and senseless near half an hour. . . . When the people were dismissed Mr. Whitefield came into the vestry, and being told of my condition he came immediately, and the first word he said to me was, "Jesus Christ has got thee at last."[25]

Marrant was carried to his sister's house, where he remained in bed without eating for three days. Since Whitefield's schedule took him out of Charleston, he sent Rev. Hall, a Baptist minister, to visit Marrant on the fourth day. After three seasons of prayer, the young man reported that "the Lord was pleased to set my soul at perfect liberty, and being filled with joy I began to praise the Lord immediately; my sorrows were turned into peace, and joy, and love."[26] Following a period of intense Bible study, Marrant devoted the rest of his life to ministry, first among the Cherokee and the enslaved in the South and later in London, Nova Scotia, and Boston.

As a result of this southern journey, Whitefield wrote a letter to the inhabitants of Maryland, Virginia, and North and South Carolina concerning their Negroes and sent it to various newspapers:

> I think that God has a quarrel with you for your abuse of and cruelty to the poor Negroes. Whether it be lawful to Christians to buy slaves, and thereby encourage the Nations from whom they are bought, to be at perpetual war with each other, I shall not take it upon me to determine; sure I am, it is sinful, when bought, to use them as bad, nay worse, than brutes; and whatever particular exceptions there may be . . . I fear, the generality of you . . . are liable to such a charge; for your slaves, I believe, work as hard if not harder than the horses whereon you ride.[27]

Although Whitefield attacked the abuses of slavery and advocated for more humane treatment of the enslaved, he was not an abolitionist. Even in the letter to the southern states, he distinguished between what might be lawful (the institution of slavery) and what was sinful (the abuse

---

25. Marrant, *Narrative*, 11.
26. Marrant, *Narrative*, 13.
27. Quoted in Creel, "*Peculiar People*," 87.

of the enslaved). In fact, Whitefield was a slave owner himself, who before the Great Awakening founded Bethesda, an orphanage for white children supported by slave labor. He insisted that slave labor was essential if the orphanage were to continue to flourish. He also owned and bought slaves until his death in 1770. By contrast, fellow Methodist minister John Wesley, in his 1743 General Rules, prohibited "the buying or selling the bodies and souls of men, women and children, with an intention to enslave them."[28]

The Great Awakening revivals and Whitefield's letter urging slave holders to provide religious instruction for their slaves, especially enslaved children, convinced some owners that conversion might make their slaves more obedient and docile. They encouraged church attendance and brought their enslaved to church, although the seating remained segregated. The Black enslaved and white owners heard the same sermons and biblical teaching and prayed in unison.

A story is told that in one church service, an old sister was shouting in the back of the church when her owner, who was in the front, looked back and said, "Shout on, there is a kitchen in heaven for you to shout in, too."[29] Although this white man attempted to put down and confine the sister's faith, slave owners were not able to control how Africans interpreted what they heard in church. After learning about the Israelites' deliverance from Egypt, the enslaved believed like the Israelites that God heard their groans and would also deliver them from bondage. After hearing the Gospels, they believed that Jesus was not a white savior but the African's Kinsman-Redeemer, who welcomed them with love and kindness. The revelation of God's sovereignty and Christ's universal love caused a spiritual awakening within the enslaved. They not only rejected Christianity as a white man's religion, but also embraced it as their own. While their eyes were blinded and their minds were shut against the white messengers of Christianity who owned and abused them, their own spiritual awakening encouraged widespread conversions.

Methodist and Baptist missions continued to grow in the South. Although it was illegal, the Methodists sent Black exhorters to work as assistants to white itinerant preachers. Because they did not insist on a well-educated clergy, the Baptists were most effective in encouraging preaching by enslaved converts. They licensed and ordained all those who demonstrated the spiritual gifts for the ministry. Black preachers ministered to

---

28. Quoted in Creel, *"Peculiar People,"* 91.
29. This oral anecdote has not been found in print.

both enslaved and mixed white-Black congregations, some of whom purchased their ministers' freedom. Some owners permitted Black preachers to conduct funerals and marriages for the enslaved on their plantations.[30]

In 1775, George Liele, an enslaved exhorter and missionary to various plantations along the Savannah River, became the first African American licensed by the Baptists to preach in Georgia. He was the first Baptist missionary, preceding William Carey, who went to India, by nearly a decade. In addition to preaching in his own church in Savannah, Rev. Liele taught and encouraged an enslaved exhorter, David George. George was appointed elder and later minister of the Silver Bluff Baptist Church, the first independent church in America under African American leadership. During the Revolutionary War, the Silver Bluff congregation joined with Rev. Liele's church in Savannah. Rev. Liele himself was evacuated with the British in 1782 to colonial Jamaica, where he built the First Baptist Church of Jamaica. David George traveled to Nova Scotia, where he ministered among a large population of Black Loyalists who had fled the colonies for freedom in Canada.

During the war, the Savannah church nurtured two more important leaders of Black churches in Georgia. The first was Andrew Bryan, whom Liele had converted before leaving the country under the Scripture, "Ye must be born again" (John 3:7, KJV). Bryan was harassed, jailed, and whipped for exhorting and gathering Black and white congregants together. He told his persecutors that he "rejoiced not only to be whipped, but *would freely suffer death for the cause of Jesus Christ*."[31] When released from jail, Bryan's owner allowed him to use his barn as a meeting place. There the church met unharrassed between sunrise and sunset each Sunday. Bryan went on to establish the First African Baptist Church of Savannah, which grew into a congregation with hundreds of members and converts, some of whom were still enslaved. The second leader was Jesse Peter (also known as Jesse Galphin) who became pastor of the Silver Bluff church after the war and later founded the Springfield First African Baptist Church in Augusta in 1793.[32]

Whitefield's Great Awakening Revival had "awakened" not just the enslaved, but more importantly the Holy Spirit who moved within the enslaved community. Whitefield himself was limited in his understanding of slavery, but the Spirit was not limited. This African Awakening inspired the rise of independent churches led by Black men and restored the enslaved's

---

30. Raboteau, *Slave Religion*, 134–35.
31. Quoted in Raboteau, *Slave Religion*, 141.
32. Creel, "*Peculiar People*," 134.

The Road to Conversion

humanity. Converts, both women and men, began interpreting and expressing Christianity using the only thing they were allowed to bring from Africa: songs and music that expressed moans of despair or shouts of joy. Common musical elements from diverse African religions merged into the worship music of African American churches. Ring shouts and spirit possession from African religions were added to their church liturgy.

Before the African Awakening, African-born and American-born slaves in different parts of colonial America were united only by vague memories of African ancestry, the Middle Passage, harsh labor, and white racism. Newly imported enslaved Africans often divided into groups that practiced varying religious rituals from their specific societies. With the increase of independent Black churches led by Black preachers, Africans in the North American colonies became a single spiritual community. They developed a distinct Christianity that became the basis of a common African American identity. It was forged by those who gained spiritual freedom, religious emancipation, and church independence before physical slavery was abolished.

Conversion and independent churches limited the owner's power over the enslaved's religious and spiritual life. In their own churches, African American believers could freely describe supernatural visions where they saw, heard, and walked with Jesus, wrestled with demons, and were "struck blind and dead in the spirit." They spontaneously composed worship songs, such as "Give Me Jesus," that expressed their personal relationship to their Lord. The verses of this song, with haunting repetitions, cycled through pain and lament:

> In the morning, when I rise,
> In the morning, when I rise,
> In the morning, when I rise, Give me Jesus.
>
> I heard my mother cry,
> I heard my mother cry,
> I heard my mother cry, Give me Jesus.
>
> I heard the mourner say,
> I heard the mourner say,
> I heard the mourner say, Give me Jesus.
>
> Dark midnight was my cry,
> Dark midnight was my cry,
> Dark midnight was my cry, Give me Jesus.

> Oh, when I come to die,
> Oh, when I come to die,
> Oh, when I come to die, Give me Jesus.

After each of these lamenting stanzas, the repeated refrain struck a defiant, triumphant, and hope-filled tone:

> Give me Jesus, give me Jesus.
> You may have all this world, just give me Jesus.

Black church leaders who learned to read the Bible from white missionaries now preached their own passionate sermons based on the word of God. They taught biblical messages and stories with music and song. As Christianity spread among the enslaved through their own preachers and leaders in their own way, enslaved Africans were no longer a mission people. They no longer needed white people to oversee their conversion, baptism, and initiation into the body of Christ. Enslaved Africans newly imported into the colonies were introduced to Christianity by African American believers. They were converted with passion and music, not with forced instruction and memorization.

At the same time, the literacy that went along with conversion enabled the enslaved to understand and claim for themselves the liberty and freedom of America's Revolutionary War. The Great Awakening revival was intended to awaken faith among colonial settlers. However, the Spirit that moved within enslaved Africans made them founders of their own religious communities and participants in the making of America's religion. Throughout the South, little negro congregations under the leadership of negro preachers sprang up wherever they were tolerated. Often they were suppressed, yet often they were privately encouraged. Not infrequently they met in secret.

One of the most unexpected outcomes from the Great Awakening was a choice made by the Wheatleys, a slave-owning white family in Boston. Inspired by Whitefield's advocacy of biblical literacy for enslaved children, the Wheatleys chose to educate an enslaved child they bought from a Boston slave market. This child became Phillis Wheatley, an African American Christian woman who expressed the ideals of the Revolution and her faith in her own words. She was the first African-born published author and the second woman to publish a book in North America. She is the subject of our next chapter.

3

Phillis Wheatley

Christian Oracle

Take him, ye Africans, he longs for you,
Impartial Saviour is his title due:
Wash'd in the fountain of redeeming blood,
You shall be sons, and kings, and priests to God.

—Phillis Wheatley[1]

AFTER THE SILENCE OF the Birthmothers and the early African converts, Phillis Wheatley, an enslaved teenage convert in colonial America, gave voice to both. Her writings, which proclaimed God's mercy amid slavery's evil, were foundational for the written testimonies of enslaved and free African American Christians. The poetic descriptions of her faith journey established the African American literary tradition.[2]

---

1. Wheatley, *Poems on Various Subjects*, 23.
2. Chapter 3 draws on the work of Bassard, *Spiritual Interrogations*; Carretta, *Phillis Wheatley*; and Gates Jr., *Trials of Phillis Wheatley*.

FAITH CONFRONTS EVIL

The Early Biography of Phillis Wheatley

Phillis Wheatley was born in 1753 in West Africa and was about seven years old when she was kidnapped, enslaved, and brought to America. She remembered her kidnapping when she wrote:

> I, young in life, by seeming cruel fate
> Was snatch'd from *Afric's* fancy'd happy seat:
> What pangs excruciating must molest,
> What sorrows labour in my parent's breast?
> Steel'd was that soul and by no misery mov'd
> That from a father seiz'd his babe belov'd:
> Such, such my case. And can I then but pray
> Others may never feel tyrannic sway?[3]

At first, the ship's captain, who was buying kidnapped Africans off the coast of Gambia for the slave trade, considered her a "refuse slave." Her age and gender made her of little value in a market that preferred robust boys, men, or adult women. But anxious to leave Africa with a full load, the little girl became part of the captain's cargo. She was probably kept unchained in the cabins of his slave ship, named the *Phillis*, along with enslaved women, while enslaved men and boys were chained below in the ship's hold.

The *Phillis* left the heat of Africa's shore and set sail on a four-month journey to New England's Boston. Nearly one in four of the enslaved Africans aboard the ship died on the way, but the child who would become Phillis Wheatley arrived in Boston Harbor around July 11, 1761. The kidnapped African girl was one of ten million Africans who survived the great suffering of the Middle Passage, and she came on what was probably the only shipment of slaves arriving in Boston in 1761. At that time, the city of Boston, the center both of British rule in the colonies and the Massachusetts' slave trade, had a population of over fifteen thousand people, fewer than a thousand of whom were Black. Of these, fewer than twenty were free.

The frail and nearly naked child, wrapped in blankets, was put on sale at a street slave market that was advertised in the local papers. She was bought for a "trifle" by Susanna Wheatley, whose husband John was a wealthy merchant, with holdings in both Boston and London. The family lived a few blocks from the Old State House in a mansion that already had both free servants and slaves. Mrs. Wheatley apparently chose Phillis intending to raise her as a domestic servant who would help care for her

---

3. Wheatley, *Poems on Various Subjects*, 74.

teenage twins, Mary and Nathaniel. She named the young child "Phillis" after the ship that had brought her from Africa.

The Wheatleys also may have viewed Phillis as a surrogate for their daughter Sarah, who had died nine years earlier at the age of seven. After the death of Mrs. Wheatley, whom Phillis described as combining the tenderness of a parent, sister, and brother and whom she deeply mourned, she wrote to her friend Obour Tanner, a fellow enslaved African woman, about her relationship with her owner:

> I was a poor little outcast & stranger when she took me in, not only into her house but I presently became, a sharer in her most tender affections. I was treated by her more like her child than her servant, no opportunity was left unimprov'd, of giving me the best of advice, but in terms how tender! how engaging! this I hope ever to keep in remembrance.[4]

The Wheatleys were followers of Methodist minister George Whitefield, who led the Great Awakening revivals and emphasized the importance of biblical literacy for the enslaved. He considered the education of enslaved children to be a Christian slave owner's mission and duty. Whitefield's beliefs inspired Susanna Wheatley to treat Phillis more like a foster child than a servant or slave. Phillis ate with the family and slept in her own bed. She became part of the Wheatley's social world, met with their guests, visited their friends, and attended their church. Phillis spent her days learning, not working, because Susanna Wheatley felt obligated to introduce Phillis to Christianity and extended the same religious instruction to this child that she gave to her own children.

Susanna also encouraged her daughter Mary to become Phillis's principal tutor. Mary included English, Latin, the Bible, classical literature, and history in Phillis's curriculum. It was a fine education for any woman of her time and an unprecedented one for an enslaved girl. Although some enslaved adults were allowed to read in order to become Christians, writing was generally discouraged, especially among women, white or Black. Hannah Mather Crocker, granddaughter of Cotton Mather, wrote that "if [white] women could even read and badly write their name it was thought enough for *them*, who by some were esteemed as only mere 'domestick animals.'"[5] Yet Phillis's intellectual growth was impressive, fueled by genius and by the Holy Spirit within her. Just four years after her arrival in Boston,

---

4. Wheatley, Letter to Obour Tanner, 21 March 1774, [1].
5. Quoted in Carretta, *Phillis Wheatley*, 38.

she wrote a letter to a Wheatley family friend, Rev. Samson Occom, a Native American Presbyterian minister who some years later would encourage her to return to Africa as "a Female Preacher to her kindred."[6]

Even as a child, the young enslaved survivor, who had witnessed so much death and dying during her kidnapping and the Middle Passage, turned her familiarity with grief into writing elegies for her neighbors. In some of these poems, Phillis seems to express her own loss and sadness. In her elegy "On the Death of a Young Lady of Five Years of Age," she wrote what could have been a message to her own African parents:

> Why then, fond parents, why these fruitless groans?
> Restrain your tears, and cease your plaintive moans.
> Freed from a world of sin, and snares, and pain,
> Why would you wish your daughter back again?
> No—bow resign'd. Let hope your grief control,
> And check the rising tumult of the soul.
> Calm in the prosperous, and adverse day,
> Adore the God who gives and takes away;
> Eye him in all, his holy name revere,
> Upright your actions, and your hearts sincere,
> Till having sail'd through life's tempestuous sea,
> And from its rocks, and boist'rous billows free,
> Yourselves, safe landed on the blissful shore,
> Shall join your happy babe to part no more.[7]

The Development of Wheatley's Poetry

When Phillis was about fourteen years old, she turned from writing elegies to composing poems in a variety of genres. A poem written when she was only fifteen, addressed to young men in training for the ministry at the University of Cambridge (later Harvard University), included a stanza that explored God's connection to African slavery and suffering:

> 'Twas not long since I left my native shore
> The land of errors, and *Egyptian* gloom:
> Father of mercy, 'twas thy gracious hand
> Brought me in safety from those dark abodes.[8]

---

6. Occom, Letter to Susanna Wheatley, 5 March 1771, [1v].
7. Wheatley, *Poems on Various Subjects*, 26.
8. Wheatley, *Poems on Various Subjects*, 15.

The next year she expanded her ideas about God's mercy in her iconic poem, "On Being Brought from Africa to America":

> 'Twas mercy brought me from my *Pagan* land,
> Taught my benighted soul to understand
> That there's a God, that there's a *Saviour* too:
> Once I redemption neither sought nor knew.
> Some view our sable race with scornful eye,
> "Their colour is a diabolic die,"
> Remember, *Christians*, *Negros*, black as *Cain*,
> May be refin'd, and join th' angelic train.[9]

Although these poems have been criticized as condoning slavery, they speak to the Christian faith of a young enslaved African convert and Middle Passage survivor. She believed her survival and arrival in America was due to God's mercy and sovereignty over human events and his plan for her and her people's redemption.

"On Being Brought from Africa to America" is not a political statement justifying the global slave trade, but rather a spiritual interpretation of the meaning of redemption and salvation. All non-Christians are pagans living in spiritual darkness, but God's mercy offers to save those who move from that darkness to the light of Christian faith. In the first part of her poem, Wheatley repeats the theological justification for slavery she may have learned from her owners and their friends, that slavery was part of God's plan for African redemption from spiritual darkness and ignorance. Those who were brought from Africa to America, like Phillis, could now receive knowledge of the saving grace of Christ. However, in the second part of the poem, young Phillis boldly chastises white Christians for viewing Black people with scorn because of their skin color. All Christians must realize that once Africans are "refin'd," that is converted, they are fully included among God's angelic family. Wheatley's views of God's mercy agreed with the biblical Joseph's conclusion about his own enslavement: "ye thought evil against me; but God meant it unto good" (Gen 50:20, KJV).

Phillis Wheatley's writings and thoughts about God's mercy and slavery would be further expanded in her future correspondence with Obour Tanner, another literate African American Christian woman, who lived in Newport, Rhode Island. Sister Obour became Phillis's most intimate friend and only known African American correspondent. In one letter, Phillis said that God's mercy had taught her understanding and knowledge about his

---

9. Wheatley, *Poems on Various Subjects*, 18.

infinite love in bringing her from a land of darkness: "Here the knowledge of the true God and eternal life are made manifest; but there, profound ignorance overshadows the land."[10]

Phillis Wheatley, George Whitefield, and the Trip to London

The Wheatley family were adherents of George Whitefield's Methodism, and his sudden death in 1770 in Newburyport, Massachusetts, came as a shock. Phillis Wheatley may have heard Whitefield preach at Old South Church in Boston, where she herself would be baptized in 1771. Susanna Wheatley corresponded with Whitefield's British patron, Selina Hastings, Countess of Huntingdon. Whitefield may even have been a guest in the Wheatley household. His death prompted Phillis to write an elegy, which became instantly popular and was printed over a dozen times as a separate "broadside" poem that was also advertised in local newspapers. Phillis Wheatley sent a copy of her poem to the countess, probably on the same ship that carried the news of Whitefield's death. The ode, "On the Death of the Rev. Mr. George Whitefield. 1770," begins:

> Hail, happy saint, on thine immortal throne,
> Possessed of glory, life, and bliss unknown;
> We hear no more the music of thy tongue,
> Thy wonted auditories [usual audience] cease to throng.
> Thy sermons in unequall'd accents flow'd,
> And ev'ry bosom with devotion glow'd;
> Thou didst in strains of eloquence refin'd
> Inflame the heart, and captivate the mind.
> Unhappy we the setting sun deplore,
> So glorious once, but ah! it shines no more.

In another stanza Phillis Wheatley reflected on Whitefield's evangelizing among Africans in America, speaking in his voice as he preached the free offer of the gospel:

> "Take him, ye *Africans*, he longs for you,
> *Impartial Saviour* is his title due:
> Wash'd in the fountain of redeeming blood,
> You shall be sons, and kings, and priests to God."[11]

---

10. Quoted in Shields, ed., *Collected Works*, 164.
11. Wheatley, *Poems on Various Subjects*, 22–23 (modernized).

These are the lines as they appeared in the Wheatley's published book of poems in 1773, but two years earlier, in a collection printed in Boston that included her eulogy, she wrote:

> If you will choose to walk in Grace's Road,
> You shall be Sons, and Kings, and Priests to God.[12]

Wheatley's revisions here and elsewhere demonstrate her ongoing desire to develop her craft of writing and her ability to do so. Even in its earlier version, this poem might have been written by an established poet, but the revision speaks more powerfully. Its writing and publication led directly to a growing fame, her own travels to London, and the future publication of her book.

Whitefield's Great Awakening revivals, which promoted the benefit of teaching and converting enslaved African children, were largely responsible for Phillis Wheatley's literacy. During the eleven years she had been enslaved, Phillis Wheatley had written enough poetry for a book. She and her owners now gathered the writings together and announced in 1772 the proposed printing by subscription of "a Collection of poems, wrote at several times, and upon various occasions, by Phillis, a Negro Girl, from the strength of her own Genius, it being but a few Years since she came to this Town an uncultivated Barbarian from *Africa*."[13] Advertising the book as "by subscription" meant that it would be financed by people who were willing to pay in advance for its publication, a common practice in the eighteenth century.

But there were those who refused to believe that a young enslaved woman could write such powerful poetry. American publishers were reluctant to publish a book by an African because the reading public and many intellectuals and philosophers believed Africans were a subhuman species who could not think nor create literature. To convince these sceptics, John Wheatley, identifying himself as her master, wrote a letter attesting to her ability that was later included in the published *Poems on Various Subjects, Religious and Moral*:

> Phillis was brought from *Africa* to *America*, in the year 1761, between seven and eight years of age. Without any assistance from school education, and by only what she was taught in the family, she, in sixteen months time from her arrival, attained the English language, to which she was an utter stranger before, to such a

---

12. Pemberton, *Heaven the Residence*, 30.
13. Quoted in Carretta, *Phillis Wheatley*, 80.

degree, as to read any, the most difficult parts of the Sacred Writings, to the great astonishment of all who heard her.

As to her writing, her own curiosity led her to it; and this she learnt in so short a time, that in the year 1765, she wrote a letter to the Rev. Mr. Occom, the *Indian* minister, while in *England*. She has a great inclination to learn the Latin tongue, and has made some progress in it. This relation is given by her master who bought her, and with whom she now lives.[14]

John Wheatley also arranged for Phillis to be tested by a tribunal of eighteen of the most respectable men in Boston, including the governor and lieutenant governor of Massachusetts, seven ordained ministers, three poets, and several Harvard professors. This panel, which later attested in writing that Phillis Wheatley was "qualified," assembled to determine whether she was the author of the poetry she had claimed to have written and also to answer the larger question, "Was a Negro capable of producing literature?"

The testing of Phillis Wheatley was more than a way to prove that she wrote a book of poetry. She was a proxy for all enslaved Africans because she was directly confronting the ideas about their barbarity and the myths of their intellectual inferiority that justified the slave system to the slave-owning class. The African-born enslaved teenage poet was being tested to prove that an African could create literature. If she authored the poetry, it proved enslaved Africans were human and perhaps should, or could, be free. On the other hand, if she did not prove to them that she wrote the poetry, her book would be viewed as a useless endeavor by a subhuman creature who could only copy or parrot white literature.

The men who questioned her knew she could write, because she had written elegies for some of their family members. But now they were being asked by John Wheatley, one of their own class, to publicly state that "his" Phillis was a literary pioneer and African genius. They needed to be sure that she had written the items in her book proposal. There is no record of the questions posed by the white male examiners to the homeschooled African girl, questions that confronted the belief system that supported African bondage. They may have questioned her as if she were a graduate student or a candidate seeking to be baptized. Her biblical knowledge and familiarity with classical literature and history referenced in her poetry was probably pursued. In the end, her answers were effective. The men who

---

14. Wheatley, *Poems on Various Subjects*, 6 (modernized).

questioned her concluded she was the author of the book of poetry. They made the following public statement:

> We whose names are under-written, do assure the world, that the poems specified in the following page [the Table of Contents], were (as we verily believe) written by Phillis, a young Negro girl, who was but a few years since, brought an uncultivated barbarian from *Africa*, and has ever since been, and now is, under the disadvantage of serving as a slave in a family in this town. She has been examined by some of the best judges, and is thought qualified to write them.[15]

Despite these testimonials, the Wheatleys were unable to convince three hundred people to subscribe to the publication of Phillis's book, three hundred being the number the American publisher thought was essential for financial success. So the Wheatleys turned their attention to England, writing letters to friends, raising subscriptions in England to supplement those from America, and enlisting the aid of Whitefield's patron, Selina Hastings, Countess of Huntingdon. Although the countess held slaves in Georgia, some of which she had inherited from Whitefield, she had also sponsored the 1772 publication of the autobiography of Ukawsaw Gronniosaw (also known as James Albert), the first slave narrative published in England. The Wheatleys sent Phillis's book manuscript to London where it arrived early in 1773. An agent secured a publisher who agreed to print the book, if a patron were found. The countess of Huntingdon now assumed that role, allowed Phillis's dedication to her to be printed in the volume, and requested an engraving of the author for the frontispiece.

Against many odds, *Poems on Various Subjects, Religious and Moral* became the first book of poetry published by a person of African descent in the English language. It marked, as one scholar has noted, "the beginning of an African-American literary tradition."[16] It included thirty-nine poems that wove together Phillis Wheatley's knowledge and faith, celebrated the wonders of the planet, and acknowledged the wisdom of ancient scholars. She mourned her neighbors in fourteen elegies and commemorated famous men in three eulogies.

The Wheatleys arranged for Phillis to go to London with their son in May 1773 to promote the book, commending her care to the countess. Susanna wrote: "Phillis being in a poor State of Health, the Physicians advise

---

15. Wheatley, *Poems on Various Subjects*, 7 (modernized).
16. Gates Jr., *Trials of Phillis Wheatley*, 31.

to the Sea Air. And as my Son is coming to England upon Some Business, and as so good an opportunity presented I thought it my duty to send her. . . . I tell Phillis to act wholly under the direction of your Ladyship." In a note of maternal concern, Susanna added, "I did not think it worth while nor did the time permit to fit her out with Clothes; but I have given her money to Buy what you think most proper for her."[17]

Phillis was officially introduced to the countess in a letter from her business representative, Richard Cary: "This will be deliver'd Your Ladyship by Phillis the Christian Poetess, whose behavior in England I Wish may be as Exemplary as its been in Boston. This appears remarkable for her Humility, Modesty and Spiritual Mindedness."[18]

Phillis Wheatley arrived in London on June 17, 1773. She was treated as a celebrity, visiting attractions and being introduced to many people who were interested in her and in her writings. She later wrote to her friend Obour Tanner that she found friends "among the Nobility and Gentry. Their Benevolent conduct toward me, the unexpected, and unmerited civility and Complaisance [courtesy] with which I was treated by all, fills me with astonishment."[19] Phillis Wheatley also met British abolitionists such as Granville Sharpe, one of her principal tour guides, who was a leader in the British courts to end slavery. His most significant victory, the Mansfield Ruling, declared that slaves brought to England could not be legally forced to return to enslavement. This ruling meant that Phillis was free in London and could not be forced to go back to America. Urged by her abolitionist friends, Phillis gained the promise from young Nathaniel Wheatley to free her when she returned from London, and she took the precaution of having her manumission papers put into writing and sent to a friend in London.

Her stay in England may have been shortened by a plea to return to America to tend to Susanna Wheatley, whose health was failing, or the plan to return in July may have been in place from the beginning of her journey. Despite its shortness, the six-week tour and the publication of her book in September, after she had returned to America, gained Phillis Wheatley an international following for her writings.

---

17. Quoted in Carretta, *Phillis Wheatley*, 95 (modernized).
18. Quoted in Carretta, *Phillis Wheatley*, 96 (modernized).
19. Wheatley, Letter to Obour Tanner, 30 October 1773, [1].

Phillis Wheatley, Free Woman

The next ten years, however, were marked by personal loss and dramatic political changes as the Revolutionary War swept across the colonies. Phillis Wheatley's trip to London helped raise her awareness about emancipation and the responsibilities of being free. She had spent her childhood writing elegies and other poems for Wheatley family friends. These included only glimpses into her own feelings and concerns. Now as a young woman, Phillis began expressing her feelings, experiences, and beliefs in correspondence with her own friends. She wrote John Thornton, a British merchant and supporter of the countess whom she met in London: "When I first arrived at home my mistress was so bad as not to be expected to live above two or three days, but through the goodness of God she is still alive but remains in a very weak & languishing Condition."[20] After Susanna Wheatley's death, Phillis wrote Thornton again, describing the full account of Susanna's exemplary Christian death and how she sat by her bedside until the end. Still shaken by this loss, Phillis wrote again, expressing her gratitude for being cared for by Susanna:

> By the great loss I have sustain'd of my best friend, I feel like One forsaken by her parent in a desolate wilderness, for such the world appears to me, wandering thus without my friendly guide.... Honor'd sir, pardon me if after the retrospect of such uncommon tenderness for thirteen years from my earliest youth—such unwearied diligence to instruct me in the principles of the true Religion, this in some degree Justifies me while I deplore my misery.[21]

Almost as an afterthought, she added:

> My old master's generous behaviour in granting me my freedom, and still so kind to me I delight to acknowledge my great obligations to him, this he did about 3 months before the death of my dear mistress & at her desire, as well as his own humanity, of which I hope ever to retain a grateful sense, and treat him with that respect which is ever due to a paternal friendship.[22]

In this letter, Phillis does not celebrate her emancipation from slavery, but immediately turns to express gratitude for being freed by her former owner, whose support she still needs.

20. Quoted in Shields, ed., *Collected Works*, 174.
21. Quoted in Shields, ed., *Collected Works*, 182–83.
22. Quoted in Shields, ed., *Collected Works*, 183–84.

Faith Confronts Evil

Three weeks after Susanna Wheatley's death, Phillis wrote of her loss to her sister in Christ, Obour Tanner, asking her to "remember me & this family in your [prayer] Closet that this afflicting dispensation—may be sanctify'd to us."[23] Their seven-year correspondence before and after Phillis's London trip reveal an affectionate and warm friendship between two African Christian women, who shared belief and hope in God's plan for Africa's Christian redemption. In the first surviving letter written on May 19, 1772, Phillis had written Obour:

> Let us rejoice in and adore the wonders of God's infinite Love in bringing us from a land semblant of darkness itself, and where the divine light of revelation (being obscur'd) is as darkness. . . . Many of our fellow creatures are pass'd by, when the bowels of divine love expanded toward us. May this goodness & long suffering of God lead us to unfeign'd repentance.[24]

Over her next years of struggles with sickness and poverty, Phillis Wheatley would increasingly depend on help from her sister in Christ, not from the Congregationalist Old South Church, where she was baptized. Obour offered her support with the practical issues of being a free African American woman living "upon her own footing"[25] after emancipation. Phillis frequently wrote Obour about her health. In a letter written in July 1772, she said that "I have been in a very poor state of health all the past winter and spring, and now reside in the country for the benefit of its more wholesome air."[26] The next year she wrote, "I am at present indispos'd by a cold. & Since my arrival have been visited by the Asthma."[27] The following year she noted, "I have been unwell the greater Part of the winter, but am much better as the Spring approaches."[28]

She also mentioned her ill health to other correspondents. To John Thornton she wrote that "it has pleas'd God to lay me on a bed of sickness, and I knew not but my death bed, but he has been graciously pleas'd to restore me in a great measure. . . . I am still very weak & the Physicians, seem

---

23. Wheatley, Letter to Obour Tanner, 21 March 1774.
24. Quoted in Shields, ed., *Collected Works*, 164–65.
25. Wheatley's description of herself in a letter to David Wooster, 18 October 1773, where she speaks of financial arrangements from the sale of her book; quoted in Shields, ed., *Collected Works*, 170.
26. Wheatley, Letter to Obour Tanner, 19 July 1772, [1].
27. Wheatley, Letter to Obour Tanner, 30 October 1773, [1].
28. Wheatley, Letter to Obour Tanner, 21 March 1774, [1].

to think there is danger of a consumption."[29] After her return from London, she wrote to Rev. Samuel Hopkins, the pastor at Obour Tanner's church, that she was "much indisposed by the return of my asthmatic complaint," so that she was unable to accept an invitation to travel to Africa with two Black missionaries, although she promised to do all she could to influence "my Christian friends and acquaintances, to promote this laudable design."[30]

Although Phillis was unable to undertake a missionary journey, she and Obour used their letters to encourage one another in their faith, quoting and applying the Bible to their own lives. In an early letter written in July 1772, just a year after Phillis had been baptized, she wrote:

> While my outward man languishes under weakness and pain, may the inward be refresh'd and strengthened more abundantly [2 Cor 4:16] by him who declar'd from heaven that his strength was made perfect in weakness [2 Cor 12:9]! . . . But pressing forward to the fix'd mark for the prize [Phil 3:14]. How happy that man who is prepar'd for that Night Wherein no man can work [John 9:4]! Let us be mindful of our high calling [Phil 3:14], continually on our guard, lest our treacherous hearts Should give the adversary an advantage over us [1 Pet 5:8].[31]

The ease with which Phillis Wheatley links similarly themed Scripture verses in a word of exhortation both demonstrates her own thorough knowledge of the Bible and her commitment to live out her Christian faith.

Phillis's letters to Obour over the last years of her life also chronicle her financial difficulties. After her childhood of comfort and an adolescence of fame, Phillis, now free and grown, was discovering that "the world is a severe schoolmaster"[32] for a woman of African descent whose life was fragile and precarious. Phillis continued to live in the Wheatley's Boston residence, because like many former enslaved Africans she was legally free but still financially tied to her former owners.

As she became more aware of freedom as part of God's plan for African redemption, she wrote to Rev. Occom:

> I have this Day received your obliging kind Epistle, and am greatly satisfied with your Reasons respecting the Negroes, and think

---

29. Quoted in Shields, ed., *Collected Works*, 163.

30. Quoted in Shields, eds., *Collected Works*, 175.

31. Wheatley, Letter to Obour Tanner, 19 July 1772, [1]; biblical references are not in the original.

32. Quoted in Shields, ed., *Collected Works*, 183.

highly reasonable what you offer in Vindication of their natural Rights.... The divine Light is chasing away the thick Darkness which broods over the Land of Africa; and the Chaos which has reigned so long, is converting into beautiful Order, and reveals more and more clearly, the glorious Dispensation of civil and religious Liberty, which are so inseparably united.... For in every human Breast, God has implanted a Principle, which we call Love of Freedom; it is impatient of Oppression, and pants for Deliverance; and by the Leave of our Modern Egyptians I will assert, that the same Principle lives in us. God grants Deliverance in his own way and Time.[33]

As she tried to gain her own footing as a self-supporting writer, Phillis Wheatley struggled to publish another book. However, she no longer had the allies and supporters who helped publish her first book. The powerful men who had attested to her authorship were either dead or no longer in Boston. The Revolutionary War caused economic stresses that prevented her London contacts from assisting her. She also recognized changes in her Boston admirers after her emancipation and the death of Susanna Wheatley, her patron and owner. Phillis wrote to John Thornton that some who "seem'd to respect me while under my mistresses patronage ... have already put on a reserve."[34] Phillis, no longer a celebrity and popular writer, had become just another free African American working woman trying to support herself during a war that was growing closer and more intense. The British occupation of Boston forced John Wheatley to transfer the bulk of his property to his son Nathaniel and move his business to Providence, Rhode Island. Phillis probably accompanied Mary Wheatley and her husband, Rev. John Lathrop, when they moved from Boston to Providence and returned to Boston with them two years later.

Shortly after returning to Boston, Phillis Wheatley became engaged to John Peters, a free Black man and shopkeeper. They married in 1778, the same year both John Wheatley and his daughter Mary died. For the first time in her life, Phillis was living with an African American. She entered a Black social world in far more turmoil and uncertainty than the wealthy white society of her upbringing. At first, this seemed like a promising change. Phillis was preparing a second volume for publication that would include letters and poetry in a book twice as long as her first. Her writing now reflected her interest in secular as well as Christian subjects. Her

---

33. Quoted in Shields, ed., *Collected Works*, 176–77.
34. Quoted in Shields, ed., *Collected Works*, 183.

poetry was moving from the personal loss recorded in elegies to national subjects and natural rights. By the end of 1779, she had a new book ready for publication. She seemed to be on the road, with her husband, to economic stability. However, like many tradesmen and shopkeepers in colonial Boston, John Peters was both a debtor and a creditor who was caught up in a cycle of suits and counter-suits that caused him financial loss. After a ruinous lawsuit in 1780, the couple was forced to move to a poorer Boston community than the one they lived in when they first married.

The fragile postwar economy also caused a decline in their finances. Phillis's difficult conditions are revealed in her brief, final letters to Obour. In May 1778, she wrote of the "uncertain duration of all things temporal" even as she begged Obour to "do me a great favour if you'll write me by every opportunity."[35] Her last letter of May 10, 1779 apologizes for her silence since "a variety of hindrances was the cause of my not writing to you," and again begs Obour not to forget her: "Pray write me soon for I long to hear from you," before concluding, "I wish you much happiness and am Dear Obour your friend & sister Phillis Peters."[36]

During these final years, John Peters struggled to make a living for his family in the postwar depression that gripped the former colonies at the conclusion of the Revolutionary War. He appears to have been in and out of prison for debt. Without kin or community, Phillis was alone in coping with poverty, illness, and the early deaths of her first children, although a niece of Susanna Wheatley may have kept in touch and tried to help her aunt's former slave. During the last years of Phillis's life, she pursued her calling as a poet, writing by candlelight in a drafty and dark room as she struggled with pregnancy, poverty, and failing health. She published only three new poems after 1776. Many others have been lost.

Phillis Wheatley, enslaved as a child with a childlike faith in God's mercy, now free and married, wrote a prayer in 1779 before the birth of one of her children. She cried out to God for mercy with all the sorrow of a woman who had already miscarried or birthed a dying child:

> Oh my Gracious Preserver! hitherto thou has brought [me,] be pleased when thou bringest to the birth to give [me] strength to bring forth living & perfect a being who shall be greatly instrumental in promoting thy [glory.] Though conceived in Sin and brought forth in iniquity yet thy infinite wisdom can bring a clean thing out

---

35. Wheatley, Letter to Obour Tanner, 29 May 1778, [1] (modernized).
36. Wheatley, Letter to Obour Tanner, 10 May 1779, [1].

of an unclean, a vessel of Honor filled for thy glory—grant me to live a life of gratitude to thee for the innumerable benefits—O Lord my God! instruct my ignorance & enlighten my Darkness. Thou art my King, take [thou] the entire possession of [all] my powers & faculties & let me be no longer under the dominion of sin—Give me a sincere & hearty repentance for all my [grievous?] offences & strengthen by thy grace my resolutions on amendment & circumspection for the time to come—Grant me [also] the spirit of Prayer and Supplication according to thy own most gracious Promises.[37]

Five years later, Phillis Wheatley Peters died when she was only thirty-one years old. Pregnancy and the asthmatic condition that had affected Phillis in previous winters may have caused or contributed to her death. Afterwards, relatives of the Wheatley family pondered the source of Phillis's genius. A great grandniece of Susanna Wheatley reflected on her abilities, given the general lack of education for women in the American colonies. She concluded that

> She had no brilliant exhibition of feminine genius before her, to excite her emulation; and we are at a loss to conjecture, how the first strivings of her mind after knowledge—her delight in literature, her success even in a dead language, the first bursting forth of her thoughts in song—can be accounted for, unless those efforts are allowed to have been inspirations of that genius which is the gift of God.[38]

This acknowledgment that Phillis Wheatley's genius was a "gift of God" was one that Phillis herself recognized and for which she gave thanks.

Phillis Wheatley's Legacy

Phillis Wheatley, the gifted Oracle whose writing became the voice of African converts, did not write in the cadence and sounds of African song. Instead, she composed her poems in the lonely, stilted voice of an enslaved African child raised and taught by an upper-class British American family. As a child, her owners closely supervised her education and writings. However, as she grew older, her deepened faith turned to reflections about

---

37. Quoted in Carretta, *Phillis Wheatley*, 185 (modernized); some scholars doubt the attribution of this prayer to Wheatley.

38. Odell, *Memoir and Poems*, 26; scholars remain skeptical regarding many of Odell's claims about the life of Phillis Wheatley.

God's plan for African redemption. Looking beyond the language and style of her poetry, her correspondence with Obour Tanner, her sister in Christ, reveals Phillis Wheatley as an African Christian believer who loved God and Africa. She believed her testimony demonstrated God's mercy and the promise of the saving change Obour had described to her. Phillis wrote, "It gives me very great pleasure to hear of so many of my nation, seeking with eagerness the way to true felicity. O may we all meet at length in that happy mansion."[39] These sisters, tied together in their hope for a Christian spiritual awakening in Africa, caused Phillis to write to Rev. Hopkins that she and Obour were living witnesses of the biblical prophecy: "Ethiopia shall soon stretch forth her hands unto God" (Ps 68:31, KJV).[40]

It is not difficult to understand Phillis Wheatley's unwavering faith in God's mercy, considering her miraculous survival and unique circumstances that allowed her to become literate and able to publish her writings. Although young and frail, she was one of the ten million Africans to survive the Middle Passage and arrive in the Americas. She was one of fewer than twenty of those survivors whose words found their way directly into print during their lifetime. She was aboard the only shipment of Africans to arrive in Boston in 1761, after nearly one in four of the enslaved Africans aboard died on the way. She was bought by one of the few slave-owning families in the colonies willing to teach enslaved children to read and write. Because of their God-inspired actions and choices, that family helped to publish her first book.

Phillis Wheatley survived the Middle Passage and the subtle, seductive forms of American slavery. God's mercy manifested itself through her, an unexplained genius who confronted evil ideas about uncivilized Africans. Although surrounded and raised by whites, Phillis Wheatley maintained her African identity and love for Africa. She often wrote as an Ethiop and Christian Oracle, delivering a divine revelation of God's mercy that implanted the love of freedom in his plan for her people's redemption. In an elegy on the death of General David Wooster, written during the difficult days of the Revolutionary War and sent to his wife Mary, Phillis Wheatley linked the American dream of liberty with the need to emancipate enslaved Africans, addressing herself first in a prayer to God and then to her fellow Americans:

---

39. Quoted in Shields, ed., *Collected Works*, 165.
40. Quoted in Shields, ed., *Collected Works*, 176.

> With thine own hand conduct them and defend
> And bring the dreadful contest to an end—
> For ever grateful let them live to thee
> And keep them ever Virtuous, brave, and free—
> But how, presumptuous shall we hope to find
> Divine acceptance with th'Almighty mind—
> While yet (O deed ungenerous!) they disgrace
> And hold in bondage Afric's blameless race;
> Let virtue reign—And those accord our prayers
> Be victory our's, and generous freedom theirs.[41]

Phillis Wheatley understood that God's plan did not justify oppressing Africans, but rather was a mysterious means for drawing all who live in the darkness of sin and ignorance to salvation's light. She prayed for Africans to join in sweet fellowship with African Christians like herself who were brought to America by God's mercy to learn of him and the power of the Christian faith. God went beyond the limits placed by white Christians on African literacy merely as a means of conversion and biblical understanding. Through God's grace, Phillis demonstrated that writing offered African Christians a means to affirm their feelings and document their bondage with another kind of African singing. The mantle of Phillis Wheatley's written faith was taken up by subsequent generations of literate African Americans—orators, journalists, preachers, revolutionaries, educators, and poets—many of whom we will encounter in the following chapters.

---

41. Wheatley, Letter to Mary Wooster, 15 July 1778, [2].

4

Hope and Despair in the New Nation

> *And it shall come to pass...*
> *that I will pour out my Spirit upon all flesh;*
> *and your sons,*
> *and your daughters shall prophecy.*
> —JOEL 2:28, KJV; EPIGRAPH FROM THE RELIGIOUS
> EXPERIENCE AND JOURNAL OF MRS. JARENA LEE[1]

FROM THE INCEPTION OF the United States, African Americans wavered between the hope of its democratic vision and the reality and despair of slavery and white racism. Free African Americans in the North, who were hopeful of salvation and religious freedom, confronted racism from white Christians as they began their own churches and religious organizations. In the southern states, religious freedom could not coexist with slavery and white political power. The deepening despair in the South caused African America Christians such as Gabriel Prosser and Denmark Vesey to believe that the Bible sanctioned their attempts to violently overthrow slavery.

---

1. Lee, *Religious Experience and Journal*, 3.

Movements toward Freedom

After the Revolutionary War and the Declaration of Independence, African American Christians hoped for an end to slavery and greater freedom in the new nation, whose revolutionary language promised equality and justice. When Congress banned the international slave trade, beginning January 1, 1808, Peter Williams Jr., a young free African American, was chosen to deliver a speech in New York City to celebrate the new law. Williams, who would later organize St. Philip's African Episcopal Church and become its first rector, offered this hopeful prayer for Africa's children as part of his abolitionist speech:

> Oh, God! we thank thee, that thou didst condescend
>   to listen to the cries of Africa's wretched sons;
>   and that thou didst interfere in their behalf.
> At thy call humanity sprang forth, and espoused the cause of the oppressed:
>   one hand she employed in drawing from their vitals
>   the deadly arrows of injustice;
>   and the other in holding a shield, to defend them from fresh assaults:
> and at that illustrious moment,
>   when the sons of 76 pronounced these United States free and independent;
>   when the spirit of patriotism, erected a temple sacred to liberty;
>   when the inspired voice of Americans first uttered those noble sentiments,
>   "we hold these truths to be self-evident, that all men are created equal;
>   that they are endowed by their Creator with certain unalienable rights;
>   among which are life, liberty, and the pursuit of happiness;"
>   and when the bleeding African, lifting his fetters, exclaimed,
>   "am I not a man and a brother;"
> then with redoubled efforts, the angel of humanity strove
>   to restore to the African race, the inherent rights of man.[2]

However, the "angel of humanity" had not restored inherent rights to African Americans. National unity and independence instead had come at the cost of merging differing political interests. In the mid-Atlantic and southern states (Virginia, Maryland, North and South Carolina, and Georgia), slavery was increasing naturally through the birth of slave children. In the free states (Pennsylvania, New York, Massachusetts, New Jersey, Connecticut, New Hampshire, Maine, and Vermont), slavery was dying out.

---

2. This prayer is embedded in an oration presented by Mr. Williams at a celebration on January 1, 1808 in New York City; Williams Jr., *Oration*, 19.

Hope and Despair in the New Nation

The representatives at the Constitutional Convention wrestled with these competing interests. In the end, they created a unified country by refusing to abolish slavery. As Thomas Jefferson noted privately during the debate, South Carolina and Georgia "had never attempted to restrain the importation of slaves" but the northern states were also not innocent. He shrewdly commented that "our Northern brethren also I believe felt a little tender under those censures; for tho' their people have few slaves themselves they have been pretty considerable carriers of them to others."[3] The Constitutional Convention also declared that, for electoral purposes, the nearly one million enslaved Africans in the country would each count as three-fifths of a person. This provision was originally intended to keep the slave-owning states from capitalizing on their enslaved populations by counting them in a census but refusing them a vote. But the notion of "three-fifths a person" was deeply offensive. In addition, the 1808 law that banned the international slave trade did not abolish domestic trading in slaves. To unite the states, revolutionary ideals were compromised by denying freedom to the still enslaved Africans. Slavery became a permanent part of the economy of the new nation.

Yet a decade after the nation's founding, free and enslaved African Americans began demonstrating the spiritual and political freedom they sought. In his autobiography, Richard Allen recounted his conversion when he was around twenty years old and still enslaved before the war:

> I was awakened and brought to see myself poor, wretched and undone, and without the mercy of God must be lost.... One night I thought hell would be my portion. I cried unto Him who delighteth to hear the prayers of a poor sinner; and all of a sudden my dungeon shook, my chains flew off, and glory to God, I cried. My soul was filled.[4]

After this experience, Allen joined a Methodist society and began to attend class meetings taught by John Gray. With his brother, he organized family prayer, which his unconverted master often attended, and he invited the Methodist minister and abolitionist Freeborn Garrison to preach at his master's house. After hearing a sermon from Daniel 5:27, "Thou art weighed in the balances, and art found wanting" (KJV), his master was convicted that it was wrong to hold slaves and proposed to the Allen brothers

---

3. Jefferson, *Papers of Thomas Jefferson*, 1:314–15.
4. Allen, *Life, Experience, and Gospel Labours*, 5. Subsequent page references to this autobiography are noted in the text.

that they buy their freedom, which they were able to do (7–8). Because they lived in a free state, they were allowed time to work and earn the cash necessary to purchase their freedom.

After the Revolutionary War, Richard Allen began to travel along the East Coast, through Delaware, New Jersey, and Pennsylvania, "striving to preach the Gospel" as a Methodist exhorter (8). In his travels, Allen met Absalom Jones, a former slave concerned about the spiritual needs of Philadelphia's African Americans. Allen and Jones joined the predominately white St. George's Methodist Church in the city where other free African American parishioners worshipped. One Sunday, these parishioners were forcibly moved from the pews on which they normally sat. When the elder leading the service said, "Let us pray," they knelt, but soon Allen "heard considerable scuffling and low talking" and looked up to see Jones and other African American members being lifted off their knees by the white trustees who said they could no longer pray there. Allen recalled that "by this time prayer was over, and we all went out of the church in a body, and they were no more plagued with us in the church" (13).

After leaving St. George's, Allen and Jones established the Free African Society, a burial society and support organization for widows and orphans that became the foundation for building an independent meeting house for African American Christians in Philadelphia. Jones went on to become an Episcopal priest, but Allen joined the Methodists, although they refused to approve his plans for a meeting house.

Like George Liele, Andrew Bryan, and other African American church founders, Allen built an independent Black church and persuaded an independent Methodist bishop to dedicate the building that became the Bethel Church of Philadelphia and later the site of the African Methodist Episcopal Church (the AME), a denomination committed to African American unity, self-determination, and freedom. However, African American freedom in the North was shadowed by slavery's persistence in the South.

Resistance and Colonization

Inspired by the American Revolution and news of a slave uprising in Haiti, enslaved Gabriel Prosser expressed his idea of American freedom by planning an armed slave rebellion near Richmond, Virginia in 1800. Gabriel and his brother Martin, a preacher, believed the enslaved should resist slavery because, like the Israelites, God intended them to be freed from bondage.

Gabriel began recruiting soldiers and amassing weapons, intending to force slave owners to free their slaves. Gabriel expected support from friendly white allies and the enslaved throughout the region. His rebel army would march under the banner "Death or Liberty," the slogan of the Haitian revolt. However, a storm postponed the planned attack, and betrayal by enslaved informants stopped the revolt before it occurred. Gabriel escaped on a boat owned by a recently converted Methodist, but was pursued, captured, and later hung with some of his followers. Other conspirators were arrested or deported from the state.

Although Gabriel remained silent during his trial, one conspirator reportedly said, "I have nothing more to offer than what General Washington would have had to offer, had he been taken by the British and put to trial by them. I have adventured my life in endeavoring to obtain the liberty of my countrymen, and am a willing sacrifice in their cause."[5]

The extent of this rebellion, the most far-reaching slave revolt in the young nation's history, forced authorities to quickly pass laws restricting unsupervised meetings of the enslaved, including church gatherings. However, laws and reprisals could not stop enslaved African Americans from interjecting themselves into the national agenda. They believed that the ideals of the American Revolution and God supported their emancipation. Successful slave revolts faced many obstacles in the United States because African Americans were divided by legal status and separated by regional distances. In slave states, the enslaved could not meet freely or organize societies. In free states, however, African Americans, like Richard Allen, could establish independent organizations and churches where they could freely discuss political issues.

In 1817, nearly three thousand African Americans met at Bethel AME church in Philadelphia to discuss one such important issue: colonization plans for free African Americans to migrate to West Africa. A year earlier, white clergyman Robert Finley and African American ship builder Paul Cuffee had begun The American Colonization Society (ACS). Finley proposed establishing colonies in Africa for free African Americans because he believed they would never integrate into American society. Cuffee, who had petitioned Congress for permission to carry African Americans to Sierra Leone, supported colonization because he believed it offered free African Americans an opportunity for trade, commerce, and social uplift they couldn't attain in the United States. Some African American clergy also

---

5. Quoted in Johnson and Smith, *Africans in America*, 256.

supported colonization because they believed it would extend Christian missions on the continent.

The meeting in 1817 was chaired by James Forten, one of the most prominent African American supporters of colonization. As reported by *The Emancipator* newspaper, when Forten called for those favoring colonization

> a complete hush was the only response, as if his listeners were taking a deep breath for a full-throated response in the negative. Forten then called for those who opposed colonization. One long, loud, tremendous "No" went up which, wrote Forten, "seemed as it would bring down the walls of the building."[6]

Many who opposed colonization wondered whether Finley and the ACS were merely trying to get rid of free African Americans in the United States by forcing them to emigrate to Africa. These free African Americans would then not be able to support the enslaved. Those against colonization asserted: "We will never separate ourselves voluntarily from the slave population of this country; they are our brethren by the ties of consanguinity [blood], of suffering and of wrong."[7] The vote against colonization was a declaration by free African Americans of their allegiance to the United States as their mother country. Their declaration also committed their churches to oppose both the sin of slavery and the slavery of sin.

Jarena Lee Preaches the Gospel

Preaching against sin attracted African American Christians like Jarena Lee to Bethel AME Church. Lee, the AME's first female exhorter, was born free in Cape May, New Jersey, in 1783. She was hired out as a servant girl when she was seven years old. As a child, she felt convicted of her sin, but not until her early twenties did she hear a Presbyterian preacher whose "description of my condition," as she later wrote, "struck me to the heart, and made me to feel in some measure, the weight of my sins, and sinful nature."[8]

Over the next three years, from 1804 to 1807, she struggled with illness and thoughts of suicide, as well as a growing understanding of God. In Philadelphia, Lee attended an English church where she felt "a wall between

---

6. Quarles, *Black Abolitionists*, 4.

7. Quoted in Harding, *There is a River*, 66.

8. Lee, *Religious Experience and Journal*, 4. Subsequent page references to this autobiography are noted in the text.

me and a communion with that people, which was higher than I could possibly see over, and seemed to make this impression upon my mind, *this is not the people for you*" (4). When she returned home, she asked the head cook about the Methodists, and agreed to attend the afternoon service at Bethel AME with her. Lee immediately concluded "this is the people to which my heart unites." When the Rev. Allen "invited such as felt a desire to flee the wrath to come," she responded. Three weeks later, her soul "was gloriously converted to God" (5).

Despite her conversion, Lee continued to struggle. She lacked assurance of her salvation. "I was the most ignorant creature in the world," she later wrote. "I did not even know that Christ had died for the sins of the world, and to save sinners" (7). A Black layperson, William Scott, taught her to pray for sanctification. When she did so, she felt a great relief and a joy that was "past description" (10).

Sometime later, she heard a voice that said, "Go preach the Gospel!" (10). Although at first she doubted this call, she soon found herself preaching in her sleep (10). Two days later, Lee went to see the Rev. Richard Allen. When she told him that God had told her to preach the gospel, he replied that although women might exhort others and hold prayer meetings, the Methodists did not allow women to preach from the pulpit. Lee was relieved, "because it removed the fear of the cross" (11).

In 1811, when she was twenty-eight years old, Jarena married Joseph Lee, the Methodist pastor at Snow Hill, about six miles from Philadelphia (13). At first she was homesick for her friends and pressured her husband to return to Philadelphia. But one night she dreamed that as she walked on a beautiful hill near a flock of sheep, a man in a white robe told her, "Joseph Lee must take care of these sheep, or the wolf will come and devour them." Immediately she recognized both her duty and her joy. "With a glad heart," she said, "[I] yielded to the right spirit in the Lord" (13).

This powerful sense of calling, responsibility, and joy remained with Lee for the rest of her life. It is reflected on every page of her autobiography. Only six years after their marriage, Joseph Lee died, leaving Jarena a widow with two small children, dependent upon the support of friends. By this time, Lee had been granted permission by the Rev. Richard Allen, who was now the bishop of the African Episcopal Methodists in America, to hold prayer meetings in her house and to "exhort," but not to preach.

One day, however, as the Rev. Richard Williams was preaching at Bethel AME Church from the book of Jonah, he "seemed to have lost the spirit."

As Lee recalled, "in the same instant, I sprang, as by altogether supernatural impulse, to my feet, when I was aided from above to give an exhortation on the very text which my brother Williams had taken." Lee told the congregation that, like Jonah, she had ignored the Lord's calling to preach the gospel. When she sat down, she feared she would be expelled from the church. But Bishop Allen rose, recounted her story of asking permission to preach eight years earlier, and said that "he now as much believed that I was called to that work, as any of the preachers present" (17).

The next Sunday she preached a sermon to five people who gathered in the house of a friend, Sister Anderson (18). Soon Lee was traveling up and down the Eastern states, preaching in houses, churches, meeting houses, court houses, camp meetings—wherever she was asked to go. She decided to forsake all "to preach the everlasting Gospel" (18). Friends took care of her surviving son, James, who at age six showed his first "religious inclinations," to his mother's delight (21).

In her first four years as a preacher, Lee traveled 1,600 miles, 211 of them on foot (36). Despite ill health throughout her life, Lee expanded her ministry northward to New York and Canada and as far west as Michigan and Ohio. She recorded the miles she traveled and the number of sermons she preached. One year she traveled 2,325 miles and preached 178 sermons (51). In another fifteen-month period, she traveled nearly 2,800 miles and preached 138 sermons. In 1835, when she was fifty-two years old, she traveled 721 miles and preached 692 sermons. The next year, she traveled 556 miles, preached 111 sermons, and began to write her autobiography (77).

Lee's autobiography reads like a modern book of Acts. It traces her itineraries and lists her sermon texts. It tells stories about the people to whom she preached: Black, white, and Indian; Methodists, Presbyterians, Lutherans, Quakers, and Deists; young and old; the enslaved and slave owners; the receptive and the resistant. She carried a written license to preach, signed by the Methodist bishop, which she used when challenged.

She encountered opposition from both church and government authorities. In one town, she "desired to speak in the colored meeting house, but the minister could not reconcile his mind to a woman preacher—he could not unite in fellowship with me even to shaking hands as Christians ought" (24). Lee was then invited to preach in a private house and, "after much persuasion," the opposing minister decided to attend the service. Lee recorded that "my friend the minister got happy, and often shouted 'Amen,' and 'as it is, sister.' We had a wonderful display of the spirit of God among us." Later they shook hands, "as Christians ought" (24). In another town, a white official tried to take her license, but the local magistrate, when he saw that the license also bore the seal of the United States, said that Lee was "highly recommended and I am bound to protect her" and sent word to her that "he did not care if I preached till I died" (36–37).

Not all opposition turned out so well. Some ministers, as well as government officials, continued to oppose her. Lee noted that after several years of preaching the opposition was so great "that I was tempted to withdraw from the Methodist Church, lest some might go into ruin by their persecutions of me," but she persisted in her ministry (24).

Lee preached to whomever would listen and pursued Christian fellowship across denominational lines. On one occasion, she met with a Presbyterian doctor, Mr. Smith, and reported that they "prayed and conversed together about Jesus and his love, and parted without meddling with each others' creeds." She then added: "Oh, I long to see the day when Christians will meet on one common platform—Jesus of Nazareth—and cease their bickering and contentions about non-essentials—when 'our Church' shall be less debated, but 'our Jesus' shall be all in all" (26). On a trip to Albany, New York, she recorded sweet fellowship with Methodist friends: "They treated me very kind; they were under the white Bishop, and I under the coloured. But the same faith, same doctrine, same Baptism, same spirit. Glory to God." In the same city she held a prayer meeting at the home of a Dutch Presbyterian woman, during which the husband became converted.

Although Jarena Lee had only three months of formal schooling, she highly valued education. Wherever she went, she encouraged the Black community to build schools and hire schoolteachers. Education, she preached, was "the proceeds of vital piety" (81), an essential part of the Christian life.

Lee also spoke against slavery, as she encountered it in the slaveholding states where she preached. She joined an anti-slavery society in New York and after hearing the speeches at one convention, she said, "my heart responded with this instruction: 'Do unto all men as you would they should do unto you;' and as we are all children of one parent, no one is justified in holding slaves. . . . Doubtless the cause is good, and I pray God to forward on the work of abolition until it fills the world, and then the gospel will have free course to every nation, and in every clime" (90).

Despite ill health, Jarena Lee continued to preach until her death in 1864. She wrote that it was " better to wear out than to rust out" and expressed her confidence that "if I lose my life for Christ's sake, I shall find it again" (97). Lee also encouraged other women to exhort, hold prayer meetings, and preach. She was one of several free African American "Sisters of the Spirit," female exhorters who preached and ministered to both white and African American Christians in border and free states during the nineteenth century.

African American Churches in the South

It was one thing for Lee and other exhorters to preach to the enslaved. It was another to build independent Black churches in the slave states. Inspired by the African American Episcopal Church in the North, leaders of Black Methodists in Charleston established an independent quarterly conference and their own African Methodist Association (the AMA).[9] They maintained internal control over their contributions and members. In 1815, however, the white Methodists abolished the quarterly conference. The AMA responded by sending Morris Brown, a prosperous and free African American shoemaker and church leader, to the AME in Philadelphia to be ordained. The white Methodists retaliated with a custody dispute over the AMA's burial ground that led to most of the African American deacons and over five thousand African American members withdrawing from Charleston's three white Methodist churches. This was considered an illegal act that prompted more repression.

The Charleston African Association organized several new churches, including the Hampstead church led by Rev. Morris Brown. In December 1817, during the first worship services, nearly five hundred members were arrested for disorderly conduct; others later "were charged with instructing slaves without the presence of whites."[10] The next year there were more arrests, and African American ministers were fined, whipped, and banished from the city. A petition by a group of free men to the legislature for permission to conduct independent religious services was denied. In 1821, the city of Charleston closed the Hampstead church. As one scholar has noted, the "abuse of their religious leaders brought home the fact that even spiritual liberty for bound and free African-Americans would be denied."[11]

---

9. Material in this section relies on Creel, "*Peculiar People*," 113–66.
10. Creel, "*Peculiar People*," 149.
11. Creel, "*Peculiar People*," 149–50.

White attacks on independent Black churches convinced church member Denmark Vesey that the fight for religious freedom and independence was bound up with the fight against slavery. Vesey was the former slave of a ship captain. He had witnessed the suffering of the enslaved forced into Charleston's slave pens. Vesey used lottery winnings to buy his freedom. He learned to read and study the Bible, and became a lay leader at the Hampstead church. When white reprisals continued, Vesey began holding secret class meetings in the church for the enslaved. He read passages from the Old Testament describing how the children of Israel were delivered by God from Egyptian bondage. Like Gabriel Prosser, Vesey believed Mosaic law and parallels between enslaved Israelites and enslaved African Americans justified a revolt against slavery. He began to formulate a plan to overthrow Charleston's slave regime, free the enslaved, and relieve the oppression of free African American Christians.

Vesey was joined by Jack Pritchard, known as Gullah Jack, an enslaved member of the Hampstead church who had been born in Africa. Although Jack was a Methodist, he also continued to practice African traditional religion. Vesey and Jack became a persuasive team who attracted and inspired other enslaved and free African Americans. Vesey had carefully planned a communication network throughout enslaved and free communities in the city and rural areas, while others trained recruits on makeshift weapons. The planned rebellion was thwarted, however, when an informant reported to the authorities.

One hundred men and women were arrested, jailed, or deported. Vesey, Gullah Jack, and more than thirty others were hung. There is evidence that white authorities exaggerated the threat to Charleston and used Vesey's plot to push further harsh measures against African Americans in Charleston. The AME churches in Charleston were suppressed and the Hampstead church building was demolished. As one historian noted, "While major plots like Vesey's presented the most obvious challenges, they were constantly sustained by thousands of nameless black people like those in Charleston who attended the execution of their leaders, who were arrested and beaten for wearing black to mourn [their deaths]."[12]

During the first decades of the United States, African American Christians inspired by the parallels between their condition and the Israelites were determined to avenge the suffering of their enslaved brethren. Free African American Christian leaders in Charleston such as Denmark Vesey

---

12. Harding, *There is a River*, 72.

and Morris Brown were inspired and encouraged by the independent African American Christians in Philadelphia to pursue religious independence. However, after Vesey's failed revolt led to his death and the suppression of African American Methodist churches in Charleston, it became evident that the slave regime's police power gave it the ability to protect white religious authorities and stop African Americans from controlling their own church property, finances, and parishioners. Although free African American Christians were building independent churches and proclaiming their hope and allegiance to the United States by rejecting colonization, freedom was still denied their brethren in slave states.

5

Hell without Fires

The Second Middle Passage

And when we're moldering in the clay,
All those will weep who love us;
But it won't be long till my Jesus come,
He sees and reigns above us.

—The Coffle Song[1]

THE SUCCESSFUL OVERTHROW OF slavery in Haiti encouraged both free and enslaved African Americans. But their joy was short lived. The United States was about to expand its own slave empire through the Louisiana Purchase. In 1803, the same year the French colonial forces surrendered in Haiti, President Thomas Jefferson completed the purchase. It transferred over eight hundred thousand square miles of land from Napoleon's France to the United States.

Prior to the Louisiana Purchase, the slave regime in the United States was confined to land between the east coast and the Appalachian Mountains. Jefferson's purchase brought the Port of New Orleans and its surrounding land under the rule of American slave owners and opened up new territories to them. The United States began to reach westward from

---

1. Blassingame, ed., *Slave Testimony*, 706.

the Eastern Seaboard and eventually included the slave states of Missouri, Kentucky, Tennessee, and Arkansas. It also reached southward to the Gulf of Mexico to include the slave states of Mississippi, Alabama, and Louisiana. By 1837, there were thirteen free states and thirteen slave states.

A few years earlier, the abolitionist David Walker reflected on this expanding slave regime:

> At the close of the first Revolution in this country, with Great Britain, there were but thirteen States in the Union, now there are twenty-four, most of which are slave-holding States, and the whites are dragging us around in chains and in handcuffs, to their new States and Territories to work their mines and farms, to enrich them and their children—and millions of them believing firmly that we being a little darker than they, were made by our Creator to be an inheritance to them and their children for ever—the same as a parcel of *brutes*.[2]

It was evident to Walker and to others that slavery in the new states and territories was more brutal than the older system. The enslaved were being dragged around in chains and handcuffs. They were living as chattel without any hope of freedom. Why had slavery become more brutal in the opening years of the nineteenth century? The answer lay in the intersection of invention, economics, and expansion: the invention of the cotton gin, the economics of cotton production, and the expansion of the country westward and southward.

The Beginning of the Second Middle Passage

Slave owners had been prospering since the invention of the cotton gin in 1794, which made growing cotton more profitable than growing tobacco. The rise of cotton plantations in the Black Belt of the South, named first for its rich dark earth and then for its many workers, increased the need for slaves. As new territories opened up, slave owners quickly occupied the rich land between the Appalachian ranges and the Mississippi River. They expanded slavery southward from the Chesapeake to the lower Mississippi valley. These owners cleared the Native American tribes from the newly acquired land and bought out independent white farmers who moved westward into the mountains. The 1838 Trail of Tears resettled the last Native

---

2. Walker, *Walker's Appeal*, 19.

American nations from the agricultural South to the "Indian Territory" that later became Oklahoma.

The growing number of slave states and newly acquired cotton plantations created the need for what is now known as the Second Middle Passage. This was a domestic slave trade that began after the abolition of the international slave trade in 1808 and continued until the Civil War. It marked one of the most cruel and devastating periods in the history of American slavery. Hundreds of thousands of African Americans from the upper South were displaced to meet labor shortages on the new plantations in the Black Belt.

At the beginning of the Second Middle Passage, some slave owners from the upper South marched west with all their slaves.[3] Others migrated with a few enslaved men to begin creating new plantations. Some owners hired agents and kidnappers to obtain slaves from the upper South to meet their needs. Owners knew what they wanted: young men and women who would work hard, bear children, and expand the slave regime. All these enslaved African Americans were now bought and sold in the country where they were born, permanently tying the fates of free and enslaved African Americans together.

Separation Stories

The first Middle Passage was a brutal sea voyage that transported millions of Africans to North and South America and the Caribbean. These Africans were unable to record their own suffering and pain. The only eyewitness accounts were those of doctors aboard the slave ships who told of their miseries. Those enslaved in the Second Middle Passage, however, were born in the United States. They were able to tell their own stories of separation and suffering to Black and white reporters. One enslaved Christian described life and work on a cotton plantation as "hell without fires."[4]

The hellishness began with brutal separations. Traders bought slaves in Maryland and Virginia at low prices to sell at higher prices to the cotton plantations in the lower South. The rising prices and demand for slaves encouraged traders to abduct slaves who had been promised freedom and

---

3. For more information on the Second Middle Passage, see Berlin, *Generations of Captivity*, 161–82.

4. Johnson, ed., *God Struck Me Dead*, 161; the narratives in this collection are anonymous and were collected in 1927–1929 by then graduate student A. P. Watson.

to kidnap free African Americans. Desperate for slaves, the traders even kidnapped children from the streets of Northern cities to work on Southern plantations. For instance, Peter Hook, a free child, was kidnapped in Philadelphia and chained in a garret with twelve other boys and two girls for six months. Eventually he was sent south and sold for $450 to a Mississippi slave owner.[5]

Many of the first captives didn't know where they were going, and they were abruptly separated from families who didn't know where they went. Charles Ball, enslaved in Maryland, said that his purchaser "ordered me to cross my hands behind, which were quickly bound with a strong cord; and then he told me that we must set out that very day for the South."[6] Ball joined fifty-one other enslaved men and women who were fitted with iron collars around their necks and marched south. Family members left behind could only grieve when loved ones were suddenly sold by their owners and disappeared into another part of the slave regime. Sudden family separations became routine for both enslaved and free families caught off guard by economic forces beyond their control or knowledge.

Betsy Crissman, born in Virginia, endured many of these separations. She was taken from her birth family at an early age and sold to an owner in Tennessee. There she married, but as she recalled, "I lived with my husband six years. Then his master took him to Alabama, and I never saw him any more."[7] In her mid-forties, she was taken to Mississippi for three years, then returned to Tennessee where she cared for nine children for another three years before returning to Mississippi. Her new owner took her as a concubine, then sold her to a man who allowed her to work and earn money. She was able to purchase her freedom for $300, a relatively modest sum since her owner was eager to escape a smallpox epidemic. However, as she reported, "Next came a severe trial. My grandchildren and their mother were likely to be sold into Louisiana, and I paid $1,600 to keep them. Next my son, their father, was likely to be sold away, and I had to buy him. I gave my bond for $1,000 with interest, which, by the time I got it paid, amounted to $1,400." Looking back at her life, Betsy said, "I don't see how I ever did it, but it was the Lord that helped me all the time."[8]

5. Blassingame, ed., *Slave Testimony*, 181–83.
6. Quoted in Johnson and Smith, *Africans in America*, 270.
7. Blassingame, ed., *Slave Testimony*, 468.
8. Blassingame, ed., *Slave Testimony*, 469.

Hell without Fires

Not everyone was able to purchase their family's freedom. Reuben Madison, also born in Virginia and enslaved in Kentucky, married a slave woman on a neighboring plantation who had been kidnapped in Maryland. They had two children. Four years later, the owner of Reuben's wife and their eight-month-old baby sold them secretly. Reuben learned of the sale after they had been shipped to a distant "Spanish territory." Denied the chance even to say goodbye, Reuben said later that "this was the severest trial of my life. . . . I mourned and cried, and would not be comforted."[9] Reuben sold rags to buy his own freedom and attempted to purchase freedom for his son who remained in Kentucky. The owner, however, refused to sell the child. Reuben then traveled to New Orleans to search for his wife, only to learn that she had died. From his own narrative, it appears that he never learned the fate of his youngest child.[10]

Reuben's wife may have been used in the New Orleans sex trade, where it was socially acceptable for young white men to maintain Black women as concubines.[11] One such young woman was Louisa Picquet, who was born in Georgia and taken to Alabama when she was fourteen years old. She was forced to work in a boarding house where she was sexually harassed by her owner. When Picquet was sold to pay his debts, her new owner bought her to New Orleans to be his concubine. Although she bore him four children, her owner never acknowledged them and pretended that Picquet was only the housekeeper. In an interview after she was freed, Picquet reflected on what this sexual slavery cost her: "When Mr. Williams told me what he bought me for I thought, now I shall be committin' adultery, and there's no chance for me, and I'll have to die and be lost. I had this trouble with my soul the whole time. I begin to pray that he might die, so that I might get religion."[12]

Although the brutality of separations was a hell without fires to be endured in this present life, many of the enslaved held to the hope that it was a hell that would someday end. One former slave remembered his "old mother spinning with tears running down her cheeks, crying about her brother who was sold and carried to Arkansas" and yet singing

> Oh my good Lord, go low in the valley to pray,
> To ease my troubling mind.[13]

9. Blassingame, ed., *Slave Testimony*, 185.
10. Blassingame, ed., *Slave Testimony*, 185–89.
11. Franklin, *From Slavery to Freedom*, 204–5.
12. Sterling, ed., *We are Your Sisters*, 24; Picquet's story is told on pages 21–22, 24.
13. Raboteau, *Slave Religion*, 258.

The Coffles

Separation was only the beginning, however, of the hell without fires that was the Second Middle Passage. Slave traders were interested in profit. They would move their human merchandise from town to town, selling a few slaves in one place and purchasing others. The enslaved were inspected and bargained over in local auction houses and makeshift jails as they traveled to Southern plantation sites. In fact, selling slaves was visible and ubiquitous in small towns and local communities and in cities throughout the East Coast. But the most notorious slave market was located in the nation's capital. The District of Columbia offered a central hub for traders working in Maryland and Virginia and easy access to the South by sea or land. It became known as "the very seat and center of the slave trade," a blight on the nation and a source of astonishment to foreign visitors.[14]

Slave traders used various means to move their captives, including cargo ships that sailed from cities in the North to New Orleans and other Southern ports. But most captives of the Second Middle Passage were force marched in a coffle, a line of people chained together. They were marched from Maryland, Virginia, and the Carolinas in the upper South to Alabama, Georgia, Mississippi, and Louisiana in the lower South.

Rev. John Sella Martin, born in North Carolina, was the son of an enslaved mother, Winnifred, and her mistress's nephew. This concubine relationship, set in place by Winnifred's mistress, was intended as a temporary arrangement until the nephew's white fiancée was old enough to marry. When the mistress realized, however, that her nephew and Winnifred had formed a genuine attachment, she sent the nephew to Virginia on business and then sold Winnifred and her two children, John and Caroline, to a slave trader. They endured a seven-week journey to Georgia.[15] In his autobiography, Rev. Martin described his mother's memories of the coffles:

> Mother has often told me of the heart-breaking scene. A long row of men chained two-and-two together, called the "coffle," and numbering about thirty persons, was the first to march from the "pen" [the traders' prison]; then came the quiet slaves—that is, those who were tame in spirit and degraded; then came the unmarried women, or those without children; after these came the children who were able to walk; and following them came mothers with their infants and young children in their arms.... When the

14. Franklin, *From Slavery to Freedom*, 177.
15. Blassingame, ed., *Slave Testimony*, 702–6.

order was given to march, it was always on such occasions accompanied by the command . . . to "strike up lively," which means that they must begin a song.[16]

The traders wanted captives to sing in order to calm the crowds who had gathered to see their loved ones and friends taken away. The captives themselves, however, often converted the song into a farewell dirge, one of which Rev. Martin recalled:

> [Chorus] Oh! fare ye well, my bonny love,
> I'm gwine away to leave you,
> A long farewell for ever love,
> Don't let our parting grieve you.
>
> The way is long before me, love,
> And all my love's behind me;
> You'll seek me down by the old gum-tree,
> But none of you will find me.
>
> I'll think of you in the cotton fields;
> I'll pray for you when resting;
> I'll look for you in every gang,
> Like the bird that's lost her nesting.
>
> I'll send you my love by the whoop-o'-will;
> The dove shall bring my sorrow;
> I leave you a drop of my heart's own blood,
> For I won't be back tomorrow.
>
> And when we're moldering in the clay,
> All those will weep who love us;
> But it won't be long till my Jesus come
> He sees and reigns above us.[17]

The Black Belt Plantations

After enduring the bitterness of separation and the brutality of the coffles, enslaved women and men arrived at last at the cotton plantations, which now dominated the lower South. One historian has called them "the shock

---

16. Blassingame, ed., *Slave Testimony*, 704–5.
17. Blassingame, ed., *Slave Testimony*, 705–6.

troops of the cotton revolution."[18] Cotton production forced the enslaved captives of the Second Middle Passage to adjust to a work regimen that differed from growing tobacco in the upper South. In the tobacco fields, they worked in small squads under a Black foreman who was supervised by the settler farmers who owned them. They were allowed days off for hunting or growing food for themselves. They also developed trade skills for the construction of sheds, wagons, barrels and other materials used in the production of tobacco.

On the cotton plantations in the Black Belt, however, the enslaved worked in gangs under hired white overseers. These overseers used whippings and threats to force enslaved men and women to do the nonstop work required to grow cotton. The planting, cultivation, and picking of cotton required little skill, but a great deal of time, so both days off and the development of trade skills fell away. Small wonder that many slaves worked from sunrise to sunset and frequently long after dark. Speaking of his female enslaved, one planter told his overseer: "Make those bitches go to at least 100 [pounds of cotton] or whip them like the devil."[19]

In plantation slave labor camps, the enslaved were tortured and brutalized to meet the international demand for cotton, which had become a main source of the new nation's wealth. The enslaved became simply human machines forced to supply the demands of businessmen in free states who processed and exported cotton for the Industrial Revolution in the Northern states and England. Each day, thousands of enslaved men, women, and children, working in the cotton fields, witnessed the brutal humiliation of beatings and punishments by white overseers who often used whipping to maintain work discipline.

Virginia-born Henry Gowans, enslaved on an Alabama cotton plantation with 130 other slaves, witnessed an overseer strip and beat enslaved women who worked too slowly. In spite of high infant mortality and miscarriages, enslaved mothers were often forced to work while pregnant or soon after delivery because owners profited from women who worked in the fields and also gave birth to more slaves. Gowans denounced the horrors of cotton-plantation slavery: "I would rather be a brute in the field, than to endure what my people have to endure, what they have endured in

---

18. Berlin, *Generations of Captivity*, 171. Although this chapter focuses on the cotton plantations, life on Southern sugar plantations was, if anything, even harsher, as Berlin documents (179–85).

19. Quoted in Berlin, *Generations of Captivity*, 179.

many parts of the slave-holding States."[20] But he also honored courageous women. Aunt Dinah, an older religious woman on the plantation, cared for the babies in the slave quarters while their mothers worked in the field. One day, when the master was away, she bravely approached the white mistress, who was herself a Christian, and complained about the overseer's abuse of the female enslaved. The mistress was able to convince her husband to set some limits on the overseer, although Gowans noted that "no interference was ever made except in this one instance."[21]

On another plantation, an enslaved Christian observed, "Women with small babies were allowed to take their babies to the field and put them under trees until nursing time. A woman had better not stop to suckle her baby until she was told to do it, else she would be beat almost to death." The woman continued, "I actually saw old man F. [the slave owner] walk through the field and, seeing a baby crying, take his stick and knock its brains out and call for the foreman to come and haul off the 'nasty black rat.' Yes, in them days it was hell without fires. This is one reason why I believe in a hell. I don't believe a just God is going to take no such man as that into his kingdom."[22]

After the Civil War, when this woman recalled her own childhood, she was amazed that she survived: "When I think back over what I came through I wonder that I am still living or that I didn't lose my mind. I was beat over the head and knocked around so much that my head and back stayed sore all the time." Despite this brutality, she held onto and grew in her Christian faith. She testified that God "has taken fear out of me. He shows me things, but they are spiritual and come from his matchless wisdom, and the world can't see nor understand them." Despite being illiterate, she was sure that God "has made me to stand up on my feet and teach the world-wise out of his wisdom that comes from on high." This enslaved woman's faith stood in contrast to her owners' way of life. While she "worked like a dog," they "did everything but say their prayers. On Sunday they usually sat around planning and plotting some devilment and meanness for us." And yet, as an old woman, she summed up her life in this way: "I was just in hell all the time. But God has led me out of it and enabled me to reap some of the blessings of his goodness. I haven't got anything, but he comforts and keeps me."[23]

20. Cott et al., eds., *Root of Bitterness*, 254.
21. Cott et al., eds., *Root of Bitterness*, 255.
22. Johnson, ed., *God Struck Me Dead*, 161.
23. Johnson, ed., *God Struck Me Dead*, 154, 156, 160, 162.

Freedom's Journal and Walker's Appeal

Stories of the suffering and brutality on cotton plantations soon began reaching the more than fifty African American abolitionist organizations in the North. These stories also prompted the 1827 launching of *Freedom's Journal*, the first African American owned and operated newspaper published in the United States. The opening editorial in the first edition of March 16, written by editors Rev. Samuel Cornish and John Russworm of New York, stated: "We wish to plead our own cause. Too long have others spoken for us. Too long has the publick been deceived by misrepresentations, in things which concern us dearly." The editorial went on to lay out the topics the *Journal* intended to discuss, including "useful knowledge of every kind, and every thing that relates to Africa." But it also stated that "we would not be unmindful of our brethren who are still in the iron fetters of bondage. They are our kindred by all the ties of nature; and though but little can be effected by us, still let our sympathies be poured forth, and our prayers in their behalf, ascend to Him who is able to succour them."[24] Although the opening editorial modestly acknowledged that the *Journal* could do "but little" for the enslaved, the subsequent 102 issues kept a relentless focus on the evils of the slave regime. The *Journal* sought to live up to its epigraph, drawn from Proverbs 14:34: "Righteousness Exalteth a Nation."

One writer for the *Journal* was David Walker, a free African American born in Wilmington, North Carolina. From an early age, he found slavery intolerable and moved to Charleston, South Carolina, at the time a center for free Black activists. He later moved to Boston and in 1829 published a religious and political manifesto against slavery. He highlighted the hypocrisy of the white Christians who supported slavery and tolerated the suffering of the enslaved. He had personally witnessed the wretched consequences of slavery, which made him determined to fight its "perverse inhumanity."

The 1829 manifesto was addressed "*To the Coloured Citizens of the World but in Particular, and Very Expressly, to Those of The United States of America.*"[25] Organized into a Preamble and Four Articles, it drew on the speeches Walker had given in Boston to defend the abolition of slavery. The *Appeal* gave context and meaning to the testimonies and treatment of the enslaved in the Black Belt South. In the Preamble, Walker wrote, "We

---

24. Cornish and Russworm, Editorial, 1.

25. Walker, *Walker's Appeal*, title page; subsequent page references are noted in the text.

Coloured People of these United States, are, the most wretched, degraded and abject set of beings that ever lived since the world began" (2). He laid the blame for this situation directly on white Christians:

> The white Christians of America, who hold us in slavery, (or, more properly speaking, pretenders to Christianity,) treat us more cruel and barbarous than any Heathen nation did any people.... They forget that God rules in the armies of heaven and among the inhabitants of the earth, having his ears continually open to the cries, tears and groans of his oppressed people; and being a just and holy Being will at one day appear fully on behalf of the oppressed, and arrest the progress of the avaricious oppressors. (2, 5)

Throughout the *Appeal*, Walker showed how slavery's brutal regime created and enforced systems of ignorance and violence. He also analyzed the self-hatred of the enslaved, who had internalized messages about being an inferior and distinct race. His *Appeal* was addressed directly to the "Coloured People" whose calling, he said, was to resist and change the slave regime.

Article 1 detailed "Our Wretchedness in Consequence of Slavery" (9). At its conclusion, Walker asked his readers: "Are we MEN!!—I ask you, O my brethren! Are we MEN? Did our Creator make us to be slaves to dust and ashes like ourselves? Are they not dying worms as well as we?... Have we any other Master but Jesus Christ alone? Is he not their Master as well as ours?—What right then, have we to obey and call any other Master, but Himself" (19–20).

In Article 2, Walker attacked "Our Wretchedness in Consequence of Ignorance" (22). Here he argued that "ignorance and treachery one against the other—a grovelling servile and abject submission to the lash of tyrants... are not the natural elements of the blacks" (24). Instead, ignorance can be and must be resisted, particularly ignorance among those who think a low station in life is all to which they can aspire. Walker argued forcibly that

> Your full glory and happiness, as well as all other coloured people under Heaven, shall never be fully consummated, but with the *entire emancipation of your enslaved brethren all over the world*.... For I believe it is the will of the Lord that our greatest happiness shall consist in working for the salvation of our whole body.... There is great work for you to do, as trifling as some of you may think of it. You have to prove to the Americans and the world that we are MEN and not *brutes,* as we have been represented, and by millions treated. (34–35)

In Article 3, "Our Wretchedness in Consequence of the Preachers of the Religion of Jesus Christ," Walker questioned the legitimacy of white Christianity (39). He told the story of a camp meeting he attended as a young man in South Carolina:

> I fixed myself in a complete position to hear the word of my Saviour and to receive such as I thought was authenticated by the Holy Scriptures; but to my no ordinary astonishment, our Reverend gentleman got up and told us (coloured people) that slaves must be obedient to their masters—must do their duty to their masters or be whipped—the whip was made for the backs of fools. etc. Here I pause for a moment, to give the world time to consider what was my surprise, to hear such preaching from a minister of my Master whose very gospel is that of peace and not of blood and whips, as this pretended preacher tried to make us believe. (44)

Walker cautioned the white slave owners: "Know this, my dear sirs, that although you treat us and our children now, as you do your domestic beast—yet the final result of all future events are known but to God Almighty alone" (43).

Article 4, "Our Wretchedness in Consequence of the Colonizing Plan" (49), took up the plan to send African Americans to Liberia.[26] Walker rejected colonization and the plans of Senator Henry Clay and his slaveholding party to decide the fate of African Americans. He asked, "Do we not belong to the Holy Ghost? What business has he or any body else, to be sending letters about the world respecting us? Can we not go where we want to, as well as other people, only if we obey the voice of the Holy Ghost?" (55). In rejecting colonization, Walker was also rejecting *Freedom's Journal*, which had come out in favor of the plan. Instead, Walker repeated Bishop Richard Allen's claim, in a letter published in *Freedom's Journal*, that the United States, not Liberia, was the inheritance of African Americans: "This land which we have watered with our *tears* and *our blood*, is now our *mother country*, and we are well satisfied to stay where wisdom abounds and the gospel is free" (65).

In laying claim to America, Walker aligned the suffering under slavery with the grievances of the Declaration of Independence. He quoted the Declaration of Independence and then asked "Now, Americans! I ask you candidly, was your sufferings under Great Britain, one hundredth part as

---

26. See chapter 4.

cruel and tyrannical as you have rendered ours under you?" (86). Walker also invoked the specter of a new war of independence:

> Remember Americans, that we must and shall be free and enlightened as you are, will you wait until we shall, under God, obtain our liberty by the crushing arm of power? Will it not be dreadful for you? I speak Americans for your good. We must and shall be free I say, in spite of you. You may do your best to keep us in wretchedness and misery, to enrich you and your children, but God will deliver us from under you. And wo, wo will be to you if we have to obtain our freedom by fighting. Throw away your fears and prejudices then, and enlighten us and treat us like men, and we will like you more than we do now hate you. (79)

The *Appeal* is a document of angry protest, the first by an African American Christian to thoroughly analyze and argue against the assumptions and political framing of slavery in the United States. It expressed Walker's anger at the treatment and condition of the enslaved and the hypocrisy of white Christians who supported slavery, white supremacy, and Black inferiority. The grievances he listed supported African American claims for citizenship in the United States and freedom for the enslaved.

Walker's direct appeal to the colored citizens of the world made it popular and widely read. The *Appeal* became a rallying point in the North that demonstrated how free African American Christians were committed to ending slavery in the South. In addition, African American sailors and supporters who traveled south distributed the *Appeal* and often read it aloud to the enslaved. White Southerners, sensing the danger of its ideas, arrested African Americans in New Orleans and other Southern cities for possessing and circulating it. Some white abolitionists and free Blacks thought it too militant, but others, both Black and white, were inspired by the *Appeal* to continue and intensify their efforts.

6

Prayer Warriors and Spiritual Warfare

Oh, freedom, oh, freedom,
Oh, freedom over me.
And before I'd be a slave
I'll be buried in my grave,
and go home to my Lord and be free.

—*African American Spiritual*

Two years after the publication of David Walker's *Appeal*, Nat Turner, an enslaved preacher and prophet in Virginia, staged the most serious violent attack on slavery in the nation's history. Turner, sold three times in his childhood, was allowed by his owner to learn to read and receive religious instruction. After he became a preacher and self-proclaimed prophet, Turner reported seeing visions of white spirits and black spirits engaged in battle. The sun, darkened with streams of blood, signaled to him a war against slavery that God called him to lead. The solar eclipse of 1831 was his sign to strike.

Faith Confronts Evil

Turner and his followers began their revolt by killing Turner's master and family on August 21. In the next twenty-four hours, sixty whites were killed, including women and children. Within a few days, state and federal troops quelled the revolt, killing over a hundred slaves and hanging many of the participants. Turner himself was captured on October 30 and executed two weeks later.[1] In the aftermath, angry white people, fearful of another uprising, randomly attacked African Americans. One enslaved woman named Charity Bowery said that "all the colored folks were afraid to pray in the time of the old prophet Nat. There was no law about it; but the whites reported it round among themselves, that if a note was heard, we should have some dreadful punishment; and after that, the low whites would fall upon any slaves they heard praying or singing a hymn, and often killed them before their masters or mistress could get to them."[2]

Responses to Turner's Revolt

There may not have been a law against praying and singing, but Turner's revolt caused white families and communities to become fearful of the danger posed by the enslaved who were growing in number. When the Virginia legislature met after the revolt, many agreed that slavery was an evil system. Some argued that the enslaved should be recolonized in Africa. Others were confident that Virginia slaves were happy and content, unlike those in the Deep South.

Senator Henry Berry, speaking for another faction, argued that "slavery is a grinding curse upon this state," a "cancer on the political body of the state of Virginia" that is "eating into her very vitals," an evil that "like a mighty avalanche . . . is rolling towards us, accumulating weight and impetus at every turn."[3] He also recognized that keeping people perpetually enslaved was impossible, "unless you can extinguish that spark of intellect which God has given them," a course of action on which some owners had engaged: "Sir, we have, as far as possible closed every avenue by which light might enter their minds; we have only to go one step further—to extinguish the capacity to see the light, and our work would be completed; they would then be reduced to the level of the beasts of the field and we should be safe." But Berry argued that it was

---

1. Franklin, *From Slavery to Freedom*, 212–13.
2. Blassingame, ed., *Slave Testimony*, 267.
3. Berry, *Speech of Henry Berry*, 2.

impossible to utterly destroy a human being's reason: "can man be in the midst of freemen, and not know what freedom is?"[4]

Despite this recognition of the enslaved's humanity and claim to freedom, Berry did not advocate for the immediate abolition of the slave regime. He, along with most other white owners, upheld the slave holder's right to retain the human property he currently owned. Berry did argue that future children born to slave women should "be entitled to their freedom on their birth." First, however, such children must serve the owners of their mothers for twenty to twenty-five years in order to repay the cost of raising them. Then they were to be hired out "to raise money to transport and settle them" outside the Commonwealth of Virginia.[5] Even this restrictive and gradual process of emancipation was not approved by the legislature. The economic grip of "King Cotton" on both the North and the South required that the slave regime continue.

Others, however, recognized the fundamental injustice of slavery and called for immediate emancipation. They continued the work David Walker had begun in his *Appeal* (see chapter 5). William Lloyd Garrison, a white Boston journalist, began publishing *The Liberator* in January 1831. In the first edition, he publicly recanted his prior commitment to gradual abolition, calling it a position "full of timidity, injustice and absurdity": "I seize this opportunity to make a full and unequivocal recantation, and thus publicly to ask pardon of my God, of my country, and of my brethren the poor slaves, for having uttered a sentiment so full of timidity, injustice and absurdity."[6] He, like Walker, now appealed to the Declaration of Independence to support his call for immediate emancipation:

> Assenting to the "self-evident truth" maintained in the American Declaration of Independence, "that all men are created equal, and endowed by their Creator with certain inalienable rights—among which are life, liberty and the pursuit of happiness," I shall strenuously contend for the immediate enfranchisement of our slave population. . . . I am aware, that many object to the severity of my language; but is there not cause for severity? I *will be* as harsh as truth, and as uncompromising as justice. On this subject, I do not wish to think, or speak, or write, with moderation. No! no! Tell a man whose house is on fire, to give a moderate alarm; tell

---

4. Berry, *Speech of Henry Berry*, 3.

5. Berry, *Speech of Henry Berry*, 5–6.

6. Garrison, "To the Public," 1; the epigraph of *The Liberator* was "Our Country is the World—Our Countrymen are Mankind."

him to moderately rescue his wife from the hands of the ravisher; tell the mother to gradually extricate her babe from the fire into which it has fallen;—but urge me not to use moderation in a cause like the present. I am in earnest—I will not equivocate—I will not excuse—I will not retreat a single inch.[7]

On September 3, in the immediate wake of Turner's revolt, Garrison returned to his call for immediate emancipation. He warned white Americans that the enslaved had been provoked to violence by the brutalities they had suffered and predicted further upheavals. He indicted both the North and the South:

> You have seen, it is to be feared, but the beginning of sorrows. All the blood which has been shed will be required at your hands. At your hands alone? No—but at the hands of the people of New-England and of all the free states. The crime of oppression is national. The south is only the agent in this guilty traffic. . . . Wo to this guilty land, unless she speedily repent of her evil doings! The blood of millions of her sons cries aloud for redress! *Immediate emancipation* can alone save her from the vengeance of Heaven, and cancel the debt of ages![8]

The Liberator, which was published weekly for thirty-five years, became a forum for writings by African Americans and news about slavery. It jump-started the founding of the American Anti-Slavery Society, led by Garrison and Frederick Douglass, and helped spur a national movement against slavery by free African Americans and white abolitionists in Northern states. It united together Bible-reading Christians who had unfettered religious freedom in the North with illiterate enslaved Christians in the South. These Northern Christians became prayer warriors who used speeches and writings to plead for the enslaved, whose conditions had worsened during the Second Middle Passage and after the Turner revolt.

The Prayer Warriors Emerge

Turner's revolt was the third in thirty years, following those led by Gabriel Prosser and Denmark Vesey.[9] All three insurrections were led by African American Christians who were inspired by God to emancipate the slaves

7. Garrison, "To the Public," 1.
8. Garrison, "Insurrection," 143.
9. See chapter 4.

and end their bondage. After each failed uprising, however, the enslaved endured violent reprisals which increased their suffering and disrupted their lives. Many slaves now lived in the Black Belt states, but the Second Middle Passage that had increased their numbers also deepened spiritual resistance to slavery on the southern plantations.

Young African Americans who had been converted in the revivals of the Great Awakenings[10] were among those who were transported to the cotton plantations. They brought their Christian convictions with them. Although the Second Middle Passage disrupted family ties and tore many young people away from their extended kinship networks in the upper South, the young enslaved now formed new family units. They also, as one historian has said, "embraced one another as brothers and sisters in Christ."[11] They looked to Christian leaders among them for instruction and encouragement.

One such lay preacher was James Smith, born in Virginia. His biographer tells us that "he felt loudly called upon to go out and labor for the salvation of souls among the slave population with whom he was identified."[12] His master was so angry that he often tied Smith up on Sundays or flogged him "until his blood would drip down at his feet."[13] Eventually, this master sold him to a planter in Georgia, who also forbade Smith to hold any religious meetings. Despite the risk, Smith began to hold singing and praying meetings in the room where he lived. When he was discovered and asked if he would promise never to pray again, in return for escaping a flogging, he replied "that he could never pledge himself to refrain from praying, though his life should be taken."[14] As a result, he was brutally beaten and chained, both during the day as he worked and at night.

Smith was not the only leader to experience opposition. Owners feared any gathering of the enslaved. Mississippi passed a law in 1822 that barred the enslaved from meeting without white supervision.[15] And yet Smith and others became spiritual warriors. They developed weapons against slavery from the faith practices of religious communities hidden within the plantation slave system. Many formed "arbors" or "hush harbors," brush tents

---

10. See chapter 2.
11. Berlin, *Generations of Captivity*, 193.
12. Blassingame, ed., *Slave Testimony*, 276.
13. Blassingame, ed., *Slave Testimony*, 277.
14. Blassingame, ed., *Slave Testimony*, 278.
15. Berlin, *Generations of Captivity*, 193.

erected within the nearby forests where they developed their own forms of worship.[16] Prayer, worship, and song became the armor that enabled the enslaved to endure daily brutality and humiliation and to preserve their humanity, agency, and courage.

Although white Christians had exposed enslaved Africans to their religious beliefs and practices, they couldn't force them to believe. Faith came to the enslaved because of personal and collective encounters with God and Christ. The enslaved understood from the Bible that they were not chattel but were like the Israelites whom God would deliver from bondage. Christ was their Kinsman-Redeemer, not a white savior.

Mattie Jackson, enslaved in Missouri, remembered her mother's faith, even when her husband was sold and separated from the family. It was the stories of the Old Testament and the presence of Christ which sustained her:

> Through all her trials and deprivations her trust and confidence was in Him who rescued his faithful followers from the fiery furnace and the lion's den, and led Moses through the Red Sea. Her trust and confidence was in Jesus. She relied on His precious promises, [and] ever found Him a present help in every time of need.[17]

Although they were unable to overthrow the slave regime, the enslaved relied on God's Spirit to give them power to confront the evil they experienced each day, to be "a present help in every time of need." Faith in God gave the enslaved weapons for waging spiritual warfare that blunted the regime's power to attack their mind, soul, and emotions. One of the most powerful weapons they used was that of prayer.

The Weapon of Prayer

Praying Jacob, enslaved in Maryland, was an example of the prayer warriors who lived throughout the slave regime. His story was told by the Rev. G. W. Offley. Offley himself was illiterate until the age of nineteen, but learned his theology from his mother and father. They taught him that "God is no respecter of persons, but gave his son to die for all, bond or free, black or white, rich or poor." They also taught him that "if God calls and sanctifies a person to do some great work, that person is immortal until his work is

---

16. Berlin, *Generations of Captivity*, 194; for more on the hush harbors, see Raboteau, *Slave Religion*, 212–19.

17. Thompson, *Story of Mattie J. Jackson*, 5.

done; that God is able and will protect him from all danger or accident in life if he is faithful to his calling or charge committed by the Lord."[18]

To illustrate God's protection and the power of prayer, Offley told the story of Praying Jacob:

> This man was a slave in the State of Maryland. His master was very cruel to his slaves. Jacob's rule was to pray three times a day, at just such an hour of the day; no matter what his work was or where he might be, he would stop and go and pray. His master has been to him and pointed his gun at him, and told him if he did not cease praying he would blow out his brains. Jacob would finish his prayer and then tell his master to shoot [and] welcome—your loss will be my gain—I have two masters, one on earth and one in heaven—master Jesus in heaven, and master Saunders on earth. I have a soul and a body; the body belongs to you, master Saunders, and the soul to master Jesus. Jesus says men ought always to pray, but you will not pray, neither do you want to have me pray. This man said in private conversation that several times he went home and drank an unusual quantity of brandy to harden his heart that he might kill him; but he never had power to strike nor shoot him, and he would freely give the world, if he had it in his possession for what he believed his Jacob to possess.... Sometimes Mr. S. would be in the field about half drunk, raging like a madman, whipping the other slaves; and when Jacob's hour would come for prayer, he would stop his horses and plough and kneel down and pray; but he could not strike the man of God.[19]

Other enslaved prayer warriors retreated to secret prayer closets and private spaces. Andrew Moss said that his mother had her own private praying ground, a thick-rooted muscadine bush, and that her prayers were often for deliverance from slavery.[20] Often the prayer warriors met together in secret meetings, despite the risks they faced from owners and overseers.

Mary Reynolds, enslaved on a cotton plantation in Louisiana, described an underground prayer meeting she attended with her family in a slave's cabin:

> We was scared of Solomon [the Black overseer].... We'd set on the floor and pray with our heads down low and sing low, but if

---

18. Offley, *Narrative of the Life and Labors*, 14.

19. Offley, *Narrative of the Life and Labors*, 15–16; Praying Jacob's story is also recounted in Raboteau, *Slave Religion*, 306.

20. Raboteau, *Slave Religion*, 219.

Faith Confronts Evil

Solomon heared he'd come and beat on the wall with the stock of his whip. He'd say "I'll come in there and tear the hide off you backs." . . . But some of the old [people] tell us we got to pray to God that He don't think different of the blacks and the whites. I know that Solomon is burning in hell today, and it pleasures me to know it.[21]

Reynolds also told of being taken with her sister Katherine to another place to sing and pray. An old man told them of a coming day when they would only be "slaves of God." Together they prayed for "the end of tribulation and the end of beatings and for shoes that fit our feet . . . [for] all we wanted to eat and special for fresh meat."[22] When she remembered her childhood as an enslaved girl, Mary recalled what she hated most: "when they'd beat me and I didn't know what they beat me for, and I hated them stripping me naked as the day I was born."[23]

One night after coming from praying with her parents and sister, Mary heard dogs and horses coming toward them. Her mother cried out, "God help us." Her parents quickly placed their daughters against a fence and told them to stand quietly: "don't move and if anyone comes near, don't breathe loud." As their parents ran into the woods, chased by the dogs, Mary and Katherine stood hand in hand, shaking but silent. The dogs passed by the girls, and the parents were able to circle back safely to their cabin. When they were reunited, Mary's mother said it was "the power of God" that saved them.[24]

Although Mary and her family escaped that night, African American Christians were routinely whipped for participating in hush harbor prayer meetings. Isaac, a slave preacher, "was flogged and his back pickled" after he preached at a secret meeting. His listeners were also flogged and "forced to tell who else was there."[25] Henry Bibb was threatened with five hundred lashes by a white deacon of the local Baptist church for attending a prayer meeting without permission.[26] Charlotte Martin said her oldest brother "was whipped to death for taking part in one of the religious ceremonies."[27]

---

21. Botkin, ed., *Lay My Burden Down*, 121.
22. Botkin, ed., *Lay My Burden Down*, 121.
23. Botkin, ed., *Lay My Burden Down*, 121–22.
24. Botkin, ed., *Lay My Burden Down*, 122.
25. Raboteau, *Slave Religion*, 215.
26. Raboteau, *Slave Religion*, 214–15.
27. Raboteau, *Slave Religion*, 215.

The network of underground churches was more than a way to escape from the brutalities of slavery. It was rather a means for creating a Christian life at odds with white rule. Many prayer warriors were willing to risk floggings at the hands of their earthly white Christian masters in order to worship their Divine Master as they saw fit.

The Weapon of Song

White Christians who perpetuated the slave regime believed that conversion would suppress their slaves' humanity and courage. It did nothing of the sort. The enslaved worshipped, prayed, and sang to a God who had created them, who saw their suffering, and who sustained them. Singing was the enslaved's shield against brain-numbing toil and torture. It was an outlet for their own rage against daily humiliation and enforced, outward docility. Singing also expressed the joy of their salvation. It brought on the Holy Spirit's presence and made hush harbor churches sacred sites.

Owners tolerated and sometimes encouraged singing by the slaves because they found singing slaves amusing. Songs sounded happy and reassured owners and overseers that the enslaved were content. However, singing solidified the ties among enslaved Christians because songs were empowered and encoded with multiple meanings. Anderson Edwards, a former slave, recalled that "We prayed a lot to be free and the Lord done heered us. We didn't have no song books and the Lord done give us our songs."[28] As God revealed songs to them, the enslaved identified with the crucified Christ because they witnessed the abuse and beating of their own brethren. The enslaved's songs became weapons of spiritual warfare.

A sung biblical message might be a protest against slavery:

> Go down, Moses
> Way down in Egypt land,
> Tell ole Pharaoh
> To let my people go.

"Joshua fit the battle of Jericho" was a war song to inspire the enslaved that city walls would tumble as a result of faith and persistent worship. Songs such as "Steal away to Jesus, I ain't got long to stay here," were both a comfort and might communicate the enslaved's instruction for escape. The

---

28. *Slaves' Resistance.*

chorus of "We are climbing Jacob's ladder," with its refrain "Soldiers of the cross" conveyed the prayer warrior's militancy.

Enslaved worshippers also created songs celebrating the joy of meeting with other believers:

> Oh, what a happy day
> When the Christian people meet,
> They shall meet to part no more.

Their communion song was also a plea for God's mercy:

> Let us break bread together on our knees.
> When I fall on my knees with my face to the rising sun
> O Lord, have mercy on me.

Their Freedom Song became the narrative the enslaved could not write and were forbidden to speak:

> Oh, freedom, oh, freedom,
> Oh, freedom over me.
> And before I'd be a slave
> I'll be buried in my grave,
> and go home to my Lord and be free.

John Andrew Jackson, whose first job as an enslaved child was to stand all day in a hot field posing as a scarecrow, remembered a song he had sung with other Christians on a cotton plantation in South Carolina:

> Old Satan told me to my face
> He'd drag my kingdom down;
> But Jesus whispered in my ears
> He'd build it up again.
>
> Oh, we'll walk and talk 'bout Jesus,
> Glory, hallelujah!
> Oh, we'll walk and talk 'bout Jesus,
> Glory to my soul.

Jackson explained that

> We used to sing this when we had seen the wicked in high places, and the servants of God suffering injustice. But when we had sung this we considered the end, and saw that they were set in slippery places. Our hymns were all we could get of real spiritual food, and yet they were blest by God to the conversion of many, and to the

building up of his saints. "Truly out of the mouths of babes and sucklings hath he perfected praise." [Matt 21:16, KJV][29]

Praying, secret fellowship, and singing became spiritual weapons protecting the enslaved's inner light from the slave regime's political economy and military might. The prayer warriors walked by faith in the unchanging God whose power superseded that of their owners and overseers. Betsy Crissman, who earned enough money to buy her own freedom and that of several family members as well as to build a church, summed up God's power: "When I look at my hands, I don't see how I ever did it, but it was the Lord that helped me all the time. . . . Let me say to every one, trust in the Lord, be good Christians, and the Lord will prosper you, for He is no respecter of persons."[30]

---

29. Jackson, *Experience of a Slave*, 37–38.
30. Blassingame, ed., *Slave Testimony*, 469.

7

The Holy Women

Sojourner Truth and Harriet Tubman

> *I believe that the oppression of injured Africa has come up
> before the Majesty of Heaven; and when our cries
> shall have reached the ears of the Most High,
> it will be a tremendous day for the people of this land;
> for strong is the arm of the Lord God Almighty.*
>
> —MARIA STEWART[1]

THE AFRICAN AMERICAN PRAYER warriors played an important role in preserving and strengthening the inner spiritual resources of those who remained enmeshed in the slave regime's brutal economy. But these prayer warriors, along with white abolitionists, also moved into more public arenas. They defied fugitive slave laws with an underground railroad of safe houses that offered sanctuary and freedom for those fleeing slavery. They mobilized support to end slavery with speeches, articles, and prayers that were published in books, pamphlets, and newspapers.

In 1833, one of the prayer warriors, Maria Stewart, a free African American abolitionist and a woman of profound religious faith, spoke at Boston's African Masonic Hall. She compared America to Babylon and

---

1. Stewart, *Meditations from the Pen*, 73.

prophesied that, like Babylon, America would come to ruin if she failed to free the enslaved:

> It appears to me that America has become like the great City of Babylon, for she has boasted in her heart: "I sit a queen, and am no widow, and shall see no sorrow!" [Rev 18:7]. She is, indeed, a seller of slaves and the souls of men; she has made the Africans drunk with the wine of her fornication; she has put them completely beneath her feet, and she means to keep them there; her right hand supports the reins of government and her left hand the wheel of power, and she is determined not to let go her grasp. But many powerful sons and daughters of Africa will shortly arise, who will put down vice and immorality among us, and declare by Him that sitteth upon the throne that they will have their rights; and if refused, I am afraid they will spread horror and devastation around. I believe that the oppression of injured Africa has come up before the Majesty of Heaven; and when our cries shall have reached the ears of the Most High, it will be a tremendous day for the people of this land; for strong is the arm of the Lord God Almighty.[2]

During the next decade, three of the most well-known enslaved African Americans, who had emancipated themselves from slavery, began their missions to destroy the brutal system. In 1841, Frederick Douglass, who had escaped from Maryland's Eastern Shore and taught himself to read and write, delivered his first speech at an anti-slavery meeting in Nantucket, Massachusetts. In 1843, Sojourner Truth, who had been living a quiet life after she escaped slavery in New York, became an outspoken abolitionist. Two years later, in 1845, Douglass published his autobiography, *The Life of Frederick Douglass, an American Slave*, describing the suffering and thoughts of the enslaved. And in 1849, Harriet Tubman, enslaved on Maryland's Eastern Shore, escaped from her owners and began her own rescue missions. Unlike Douglass, the two women were illiterate and could not write about their experiences. However, Sojourner's speeches and sermons were documented for nearly thirty years by abolitionist supporters such as Olive Gilbert, Frances Titus, and Harriet Beecher Stowe. Harriet Tubman's work was documented during her lifetime by Sarah H. Bradford.

Although Harriet Tubman was younger than Sojourner Truth and was enslaved in a different place and time, they both opposed slavery and shared the belief that their actions were directed by God. The faith of these Holy Women came from their enslaved Christian parents and the inspiration of

---

2. Stewart, *Meditations from the Pen*, 72–73.

God, not from formal religious instruction. Indeed, the religion they heard from many white Christians, including their cruel owners, differed from their own faith, which inspired them to declare opposition to the entire slave regime. Many enslaved people escaped from slavery before them and others prayed for its end, but Truth and Tubman were the most consistent and daring in their missions to abolish slavery. Because these two Holy Women had faith, their spiritual weapons of sojourning for truth and leading slaves to freedom were used by God to help destroy the slave regime's enormity and power.

Sojourning for Truth

Sojourner Truth was born Isabella Bomefree in 1797 in Ulster County, New York.[3] She was one of the youngest children of Dutch-speaking enslaved parents, James Bomefree and Betsy Mau Mau Bett, who were owned by the Ardinburgh family. The name "Bomefree," which meant "tree" in the Low Dutch of the slaveholders, was given to her father because he was straight and tall (15). As a young child, she quickly learned the cruelty of slavery. Several of her older siblings were sold away when they were still young children. She also learned of her mother's faith. One day she asked, "What ails you, mau-mau?" Her mother replied, "Oh, a good deal ails me." Then she pointed to the stars. "Those are the same stars, and that is the same moon, that look down upon your brothers and sisters, and which they see as they look up to them, though they are ever so far away from us, and each other" (18). In the evening, Sojourner recalled, her mother would sit down and teach her children about God. "There is a God, who hears and sees you, . . . and when you are beaten, or cruelly treated, or fall into any trouble, you must ask help of him, and he will always hear and help you" (17).

Isabella soon had need of that lesson. When she was nine years old, she was separated from her parents and sold at auction to the Nealy family, who physically abused her with overwork, beatings, and deprivation. She further suffered from a language barrier since her owners spoke only English, while she knew only Dutch. "If they sent me for a frying-pan, not knowing what they meant, perhaps I carried them the pot-hooks and trammels [hoppers for a small mill]. Then, oh! how angry mistress would

---

3. This account of Sojourner Truth's life relies on *Narrative of Sojourner Truth*. Page numbers in the text refer to the *Narrative*; speeches written in dialect are transcribed. Readers may also wish to consult Painter, *Sojourner Truth*.

be with me!" (26). One Sunday morning, Mr. Nealy beat her so severely with a bundle of rods that she bore the lacerating scars to her dying day. And yet, Isabella continued to trust in God. As she later recalled, "though it seems *curious*, I do not remember ever asking for any thing but what I got it.... When I got beaten, I never knew it long enough beforehand to pray; and I always thought if I only had *had* time to pray to God for help, I should have escaped the beating" (27).

Isabella did pray to see her father, and when he came for a short visit, asked him to get her "a new and better place" (28). The answer came in the form of Mr. Scriver, who bought Isabella for $105 and allowed her to live for about eighteen months "devoid of hardship or terror" (29). However, in 1810 she was sold to the Dumont family. Mr. Dumont was a man of "kind feelings," as Isabella recalled somewhat satirically, who "treated his slaves with all the consideration he did his *other* animals, and *more*, perhaps." Mrs. Dumont, however, was a harsh mistress (29). Under these circumstances, Isabella developed a fierce loyalty to Mr. Dumont, to the extent of believing that slavery was "right and honorable," a position that she later viewed with "utter astonishment, at the absurdity of the claims so arrogantly set up by the masters, over beings designed by God to be as free as kings" (33–34). Yet that loyalty developed an integrity of spirit that Isabella recognized as forming in her "a character that loved truth, and hated a lie" (34). She gave credit to God both for working good in her in the midst of a wicked regime and for opening her eyes to the arrogant absurdity of that wicked system.

Over the next years as Isabella grew into adulthood, she was married to a man, Thomas, who was also enslaved by the Dumonts, and together they had five children. Although she refused to detail all her sufferings, it seems probable from her reticence that she was sexually as well as physically abused during the years of her enslavement. As she grew older, however, she began to anticipate her emancipation. The State of New York had set July 4, 1827 as the date on which slavery would be abolished within its jurisdiction, but Mr. Dumont had promised Isabella that she would gain her freedom a year earlier. When Independence Day 1826 arrived, however, he refused to give her the papers that would guarantee her freedom. But Isabella determined to step out on her own, even though, as she told God, she was "afraid to go in the night and in the day everybody would see her" (41). Then, as the thought came that she should set out at dawn, she immediately gave thanks to God for his answer. Leaving her husband and older children behind, she walked away from the Dumont farm with only her infant and a small bundle of clothes. As she traveled, she asked God for guidance and was directed first to the home of Levi Rowe and then to the Van Wageners, who were willing to shelter and employ her. When Mr. Dumont appeared to reclaim his property, Isabella stoutly resisted, and, despite their total opposition to slavery, the Van Wageners paid $25 to Mr. Dumont to prevent him from forcibly taking Isabella and her child back into slavery.

Neither Isabella nor the Van Wageners, however, were able to prevent the sale of her five-year-old son into slavery in Alabama. The child had been sold, even before Isabella left the Dumont family, to a doctor in New York City. He, in turn, sold the boy to a relative who took him south. By law, the child was not allowed to be sold out of state and should have been emancipated in 1827, along with all the other enslaved in New York. When she learned of the fraudulent sale, Isabella marched back to the Dumonts to demand the recovery of her son. When Mrs. Dumont dismissed her claim and scorned her lack of resources, Isabella replied, "*I'll have my child again.* . . . I have no money, but God has enough." As she said later, "I was sure God would help me to get him. Why, I felt so *tall within*—I felt as if the power of a nation was with me!" (45).

This utter confidence in God's provision never deserted Isabella, but it also motivated her to do everything in her power to free her child. After she prayed, "O Lord, give my son into my hands, and that speedily! Let not the spoilers have him any longer" (50), she did not sit down and wait for an angel to rescue him. Instead, she persistently sought advocates among the Quakers, pressured the law courts, raised money for a barrister to locate and ransom young Peter, and refused to give up even when she felt that she had "wearied" all her friends. When they were finally reunited, Peter refused at first to recognize her, traumatized as he was by the incessant cruelty that had broken his body and almost his spirit. But Isabella was able to draw him back into her care, even as she lamented the torment he had undergone.

As a young adult, Isabella began a habit of prayers, or "talks with God," spoken aloud in the outdoors. She had the feeling that if she spoke very loudly, under the open skies, God would more readily hear her. So she found an island in a small stream, covered with willows, where she could pray without fear of being overheard or seen. Here she demanded that God protect her from evil and send her to a kind mistress, in payment for which she promised to be good "*all* of the time" (62). But she soon realized two things: she could not be good all of the time and when she found herself with a relatively pleasant life, working for the Van

Wageners, she no longer felt she needed to turn to God, "who was only known to her as a help in trouble" (62).

One day, as she was preparing to celebrate a holiday with friends, God suddenly revealed himself as the one who was "*all over* . . . and that there was no place where God was not" (65). She was instantly aware of her broken promises and her sin in forgetting God. Where could she flee from God's presence? How could she survive if he looked at her again? She abandoned her plans to attend the party, walked back into the house, and tried to pray. But she could not. "What! Shall I lie again to God? I have told him nothing but lies; and shall I speak again, and tell another lie to God?" (66). In this state of great distress, she began to wish for a mediator and gradually she felt that a friend was standing between herself and God. Who was this person? She felt that she both knew him and didn't know him. As her biographer recounts, "'Who are you?' was the cry of her heart. . . . At length, after bending both soul and body with the intensity of this desire, till breath and strength seemed failing, and she could maintain her position no longer, an answer came to her, saying distinctly, 'It is Jesus.' 'Yes,' she responded, 'it is *Jesus.*'" (67). From this time on, her confidence in God's provision and in the power of prayer was strengthened by her assurance that Jesus was her friend, "through whom, love flowed as from a fountain" (69). It was this encounter with Jesus that allowed her to love "*even the white folks*" who had abused her and her people. As she testified, "I knew it—I felt it. Jesus was my Jesus. Jesus would love me always" (159).

Isabella needed that confidence in the difficult years that followed her emancipation. Her elderly husband, who chose to remain with the Dumonts, died. Isabella, with two of her children, moved to New York City, where she found work as a domestic servant for some time in the household of religious extremists who considered themselves prophets and who eventually stole all her savings. Peter, the ransomed son, fell in with a bad crowd, was sent to sea, and disappeared. In the city, however, Isabella also found spiritual companionship in both white and Black churches and was reunited with siblings whom she had never met or had not seen for years.

In 1843, however, Isabella felt called to leave New York City, travel east, and lecture—"testifying of the hope that was in her" (101)—despite having no contacts outside the city and few resources. When her landlady asked why she was leaving, Isabella answered that her name was now "Sojourner" and "The Spirit calls me there, and I must go" (100). As she later told the writer Harriet Beecher Stowe,

> When I left the house of bondage, I left everything behind. I wasn't going to keep nothing of Egypt on me, and so I went to the Lord and asked him to give me a new name. And the Lord gave me Sojourner, because I was to travel up and down the land, showing the people their sins, and being a sign unto them. Afterward I told the Lord I wanted another name, because everybody else had two names; and the Lord gave me Truth, because I was to declare the truth to the people. (164)

As Sojourner traveled and testified, she continued to develop her understanding of God. Although she never learned to read, she was a student of the Bible, but preferred to have it read to her by children, since they were willing to reread passages word-for-word, so that she could meditate on the meaning. Adults, on the other hand, tended to read a passage once and then try to explain it, rather than simply rereading it to her (108). At camp meetings and other gatherings, she became a favorite guest. One friend wrote, "Many were the lessons of wisdom and faith I have delighted to learn from her. . . . She continued a great favorite in our meetings, both on account of her remarkable gift in prayer, and still more remarkable talent for singing" (114).

The year 1851 marked a turning point in Sojourner's life. She joined a lecture tour with other abolitionists traveling throughout western New York. As her biographer noted, "To advocate the cause of the enslaved at this period was both unpopular and unsafe. Their meetings were frequently disturbed or broken up by the pro-slavery mob, and their lives imperiled" (131). Later that year, she delivered her famous "Ain't I a Woman?" speech to a Woman's Rights Convention in Akron, Ohio. Responding to two days of speeches from men who questioned the equality of women, she said:

> That man over there says that women need to be helped into carriages, and lifted over ditches, and to have the best place everywhere. Nobody ever helps me into carriages, or over mud puddles, or gives me any best place . . . and ar'n't I a woman? Look at me! Look at my arm! . . . I have plowed, and planted, and gathered into barns, and no man could head [outdo] me—and ar'n't I a woman? I could work as much and eat as much as a man (when I could get it), and bear the lash as well—and ar'n't I a woman? I have borne thirteen children and seen them most all sold off into slavery, and when I cried out with a mother's grief, none but Jesus heard—and ar'n't I a woman? (134)[4]

---

4. Sojourner, who had five children of her own, apparently incorporated her mother

She then turned to a minister who had argued that women did not have as many rights as a man because Christ was not a woman. To which she replied, "Where did your Christ come from? From God and a woman. Man had nothing to do with him" (135).

The impact of this speech was enormous, with listeners recognizing that Sojourner spoke the truth about the humanity of enslaved women and, indeed, the humanity of every woman. As one female member of the audience later wrote, "She had taken us up in her strong arms and carried us safely over the slough of difficulty, turning the whole tide in our favor" (135). Indeed, the strong arms of Sojourner Truth's unwavering faith, confidence, and powerful rhetoric became her hallmark, along with her commitment to nonviolence. Once, when she shared a stage with Frederick Douglass, he ended his speech with a call to arms. The Black race, he said, "must come to blood; they must fight for themselves and redeem themselves, or it would never be done." To which Sojourner simply, but resonantly, replied, "Frederick, *is God dead*?" (168). On another occasion, she put an arrogant white man in his place with her deadpan humor. When he chided her, "Old woman, do you think that your talk about slavery does any good? Do you suppose people care what you say? Why, I don't care any more for your talk than I do for the bite of a flea," she quickly retorted, "Perhaps not, but, the Lord willing, I'll keep you scratching" (312).

Sojourner Truth did indeed keep people scratching. As she herself told Stowe, "The Lord has made me a sign unto this nation, and I go round testifying, and showing on them their sins against my people" (152). After 1856, she made her home in Michigan, near Battle Creek, but continued to travel and lecture in anti-slavery meetings despite persistent and often violent opposition. Her younger contemporary, Harriet Tubman, the other Holy Woman of faith in the struggle against slavery, spoke occasionally at anti-slavery meetings, but is remembered more as a woman of action than of words.

Harriet Tubman and the Underground Railroad to Freedom

Harriet Tubman was born Araminta Ross, probably in 1822, to enslaved parents Benjamin Ross and Harriet ("Rit") Greene, who lived in Dorchester

---

and perhaps others' experiences when she referred to thirteen children, or the number may have been mistakenly transcribed.

The Holy Women

County, on Maryland's Eastern Shore (73).[5] She and her family of eight siblings were shifted between plantations owned by Anthony Thompson, who owned Ben, and his stepson Edward Brodess, who owned Rit.[6] The county itself was a trading hub between the free states to the north of Maryland and the slave states to its south. Its several rivers and waterways were connected to Baltimore and Philadelphia.

While still a child, Araminta was hired out to work for nearby families. This was a common practice. As her modern biographer has noted:

> For a small planter such as Brodess . . . slave children appeared to have been a burden, possibly seen as a distraction for their more useful and productive slave mother. By hiring out his excess slaves, Brodess was able to maintain his social status within the community and feed his own growing family of eight children without the added responsibility of providing for troublesome, and hungry, slave children.[7]

Tubman was six or seven when she was first hired out to James Cook, a planter of limited means who lived on a nearby farm. Cook gave her the task of watching his muskrat traps, which involved wading in cold water. When she became seriously ill with measles, her mother was allowed to take her home for a time, but she was soon returned to the Cooks.

Mrs. Cook, a weaver, attempted to teach Araminta her trade, but the young girl hated being forced to live in the house. For some time she served another cruel mistress, Miss Susan. Araminta was whipped when she made mistakes cleaning a room, once five times before breakfast; she was also whipped if she fell asleep while caring for a sick child (13). In fact, the mistress actually slept with a whip under her pillow, having been taught to believe "that a slave could be taught to do nothing, and would do nothing but under the sting of the whip" (10).

In her early teens, Araminta was hired out to another family as a field hand. Details of the following story vary, but it appears that in the course of an altercation between an overseer and an enslaved man who had gone

---

5. This account of Harriet Tubman's life relies on Bradford, *Scenes in the Life*. Page numbers in the text refer to *Scenes*; speeches written in dialect are transcribed. Although modern historians are critical of some elements of this earliest biography, it remains an important source for Tubman's own viewpoints. Readers may also wish to consult the revision published by Bradford, *Harriet, The Moses of Her People*, and the modern biography by Larson, *Bound for the Promised Land*.

6. Larson, *Bound for the Promised Land*, xvi.

7. Larson, *Bound for the Promised Land*, 29.

FAITH CONFRONTS EVIL

to a village store, Araminta refused to help the overseer capture her fellow enslaved and, in fact, stood in the doorway to prevent his pursuing the fugitive. The overseer threw a two-pound weight from the counter, intending to stop the man from fleeing, but instead hit Araminta in the head, causing a severe injury. As a result, she suffered from headaches, lethargy, and other neurological symptoms for the rest of her life (74–75).[8]

Araminta was able to earn some money of her own by hiring her time to do the hard outdoor labor usually performed by men (75). Around 1844, she married a free Black named John Tubman, but they had no children. As the decade wore on, Araminta and her family became increasingly concerned about their status. From Christmas 1848 until the following March, Araminta prayed relentlessly, with a keen sense of foreboding that she was about to be sold. She pleaded with God to deliver her from Edward Brodess. "Oh Lord," she prayed, "convert master! Oh Lord, change that man's heart" (14). Her prayers grew more urgent as Brodess brought potential buyers to look at her. She feared that she and her brothers and sisters were not simply going to be sold but would be auctioned to a chain gang, going to the cotton and rice fields of the South. As the situation became more dire, Araminta prayed, "Oh Lord, if you ain't never going to change that man's heart, kill him, Lord, and take him out of the way" (15). Apparently the Lord heard her prayer, and Edward Brodess died in March 1849, in Araminta's words, "just as he lived" (15).

Unfortunately, however, his death catapulted Araminta into a situation even more dire. She learned that, despite the provisions of a previous will that his slaves be granted freedom, the executors of the estate had determined to sell them as property to pay Brodess's many debts. Legally they were not allowed to be sold out of the State of Maryland, but the enslaved had little confidence either in the family that owned them or in the court system. Although some of Araminta's family were satisfied to remain enslaved, if they could stay in their homes, this "promise" of slavery in Maryland was not enough for Araminta. She resolved not to be sold.

In September 1849, Araminta and her two brothers, Ben and Henry, ran away, but the brothers soon returned home, dragging their sister with them.[9] Early in October, however, Araminta fled again, this time alone

---

8. Larson suggests that Harriet suffered from temporal lobe epilepsy; *Bound for the Promised Land*, 43.

9. Larson, *Bound for the Promised Land*, 77–78.

with the North Star and God as her only guiding points. As she left, she sang a farewell and left a musical message for her family:

> I'll meet you in the morning,
> Safe in the promised land,
> On the other side of Jordan,
> Bound for the promised land. (19)

As her modern biographer notes, "The exact route and the identities of those who helped her remains a matter of great speculation," but she was undoubtedly helped by the Quakers and by the network that had already become known as the Underground Railroad.[10] When she crossed the line into the North, Araminta recalled that "I looked at my hands to see if I was the same person. There was such a glory over every thing; the sun came like gold through the trees, and over the fields, and I felt like I was in Heaven" (19). It may have felt like heaven, but it also felt lonely: "I had crossed the line," she remembered,

> I was free; but there was no one to welcome me to the land of freedom. I was a stranger in a strange land; and my home, after all, was down in Maryland; because my father, my mother, my brothers, and sisters, and friends were there. But I was free, and they should be free. I would make a home in the North and bring them there, God helping me.... I said to the Lord, "I'm going to hold steady onto you, and I know you'll see me through." (20)

When Araminta arrived in Philadelphia, she found both work and friends, and she dropped her given name to take on that of her mother: "Harriet." She soon determined to return to Maryland to rescue her husband and other relatives. When she discovered that her husband had married another woman and was unwilling to come north with her, her early biographer wrote that "she did not give way to rage or grief, but collected a party of fugitives and brought them safely to Philadelphia" (77). She was willing to lead whomever was willing to follow.

Although it is difficult to trace exactly how many journeys she made back to the slave state, probably around thirteen,[11] she became well known enough to warrant a $12,000 reward for her capture (21).[12] She worked

---

10. Larson, *Bound for the Promised Land*, 80.

11. Larson estimates the number of trips at thirteen and the number of freed slaves at seventy; *Bound for the Promised Land*, xvii.

12. One contemporary newspaper article put the reward at $40,000, an exaggerated sum; Bradford, *Scenes in the Life*, 22.

out a strategy of leaving with her group of fugitives on a Saturday night, because owners were not allowed to send out advertisements about escaped slaves on a Sunday. This gave Tubman and her group the advantage of one day's journey (21). They traveled by night and slept during the day and often employed disguises, including dressing the men as women and the women as boys. A crying infant might be given opium to keep it quiet. Once a group began the journey, Harriet insisted on a militant discipline and, if necessary, used force to keep her party on the move. If someone—exhausted, bleeding, fearful—sat down on the path, she would point her revolver at their head: "Dead negroes tell no tales. Go on or die." And so, her biographer concludes, "she compelled them to drag their weary limbs on their northward journey" (25).

At times she left her group to find food. To signal her return, she taught them to recognize a musical code. If they heard the hymn that began

> Hail, oh hail ye happy spirits,
> Death no more shall make you fear,
> No grief nor sorrow, pain nor anguish
> Shall no more distress you there,

they would know that she was nearby. But they were not to come out of their hiding place until she sang it a second time, indicating that the coast was clear. On the other hand, if they heard her singing

> Moses go down in Egypt,
> Till ole Pharoah let me go;
> Hadn't been for Adam's fall,
> Shouldn't have to died at all,

then they would understand that danger was nearby and would remain hidden (26–27).

There were many times when Harriet had to think and act quickly. Once she was interrupted on her way south by a young woman, Tilly, whose fiancé had already successfully escaped to the North and who now pleaded with Harriet for help to reach Baltimore, where she had friends. They hid for twenty-four hours and then walked down to the Chesapeake Bay, where Harriet expected to hand her charge over to a sympathetic boat captain. The boat, however, had been disabled. Regardless, Harriet walked boldly along the dock to another boat, joined the queue of ticket-holders, and presented a note from friends that promised them safe passage on the now-disabled vessel. The clerk told them to wait. As Tilly hovered anxiously, Harriet began to pray. Her biographer recounted what happened next:

> "Oh, Lord! You've been with me in six troubles, don't desert me in the seventh!"
>
> "Moses! Moses!" cried Tilly, pulling her by the sleeve. "Do go and see if you can't get tickets now."
>
> "Oh, Lord! You've been with me in six troubles, don't desert me in the seventh." . . .
>
> Tilly exclaimed: "Oh, Moses! the man is coming. What shall we do?"
>
> "Oh, Lord, you've been with me in six troubles!"
>
> Here the clerk touched her on the shoulder, and Tilly thought their time had come, but all he said was: "You can come now and get your tickets," and their troubles were over.[13]

When her biographer expressed astonishment at her courage, Harriet responded, "It wasn't me, it was the Lord! Just so long as he wanted to use me, he would take care of me and when he didn't want me no longer I was ready to go; I always told him, 'I'm going to hold steady on to you, and you've got to see me through.'"[14]

Although Harriet benefitted from her knowledge of Maryland, its backcountry and waterways, and from the financial and physical assistance given by abolitionists, particularly in the Quaker community, each journey was fraught with danger. The passage of the Fugitive Slave Act in 1850 meant that Northern cities were no longer havens of refuge for the former enslaved. The act stipulated that all captured fugitives be returned to their owners, and it required both citizens and officials in free states to cooperate. As a consequence, Harriet was forced to lead her band further northward into Canada where "they earned their bread by chopping wood in the snows of a Canadian forest; they were frost-bitten, hungry, and naked. . . . [Harriet] worked for them, begged for them, prayed for them . . . and carried them by the help of God through the hard winter" (77).

As she continued her expeditions into Maryland, Harriet came to be known as "Moses," in recognition of her leadership in "carrying away some of the oppressed" (78). Although a large reward was offered for her capture, she was never apprehended. She herself attributed her safety to the visions and directions that God granted her. Abolitionist Thomas Garrett wrote

---

13. Bradford, *Harriet, The Moses of Her People*, 60.
14. Bradford, *Harriet, The Moses of Her People*, 61.

that Harriet Tubman "had more confidence in the voice of God, as spoken direct to her soul. She has frequently told me that she talked with God, and he talked with her every day of her life . . . [for] she never ventured only where God sent her, and her faith in a Supreme Power was truly great" (49). He offered one story to demonstrate this faith:

> In one instance, when she had two stout men with her . . . she said that God told her to stop, which she did; and then asked him what she must do. He told her to leave the road, and turn to the left; she obeyed, and soon came to a small stream of tide water; there was no boat, no bridge; she again inquired of her Guide what she was to do. She was told to go through. It was cold, in the month of March; but having confidence in her Guide, she went in; the water came up to her arm-pits; the men refused to follow till they saw her safe on the opposite shore. (50)

The men did eventually follow and reached safety. In fact, as Garrett testified, "No slave who placed himself under her care, was ever arrested" (50).

Harriet may have been guided by visions, which sometimes made those around her uneasy. But she was practical and clear-eyed about the evils of slavery. When her friends in Philadelphia wanted to take her to see the play *Uncle Tom's Cabin*, she replied,

> No. I haven't got no heart to go and see the sufferings of my people played on the stage. I've heard "Uncle Tom's Cabin" read, and I tell you Mrs. Stowe's pen hasn't begun to paint what slavery is as I have seen it at the far South. I've seen the real thing, and I don't want to see it on no stage or in no theater. (22)

In 1857, after having rescued many of the younger enslaved, Harriet Tubman went back to Maryland to get her aged parents. She hired a rickety makeshift wagon for them made simply of a pair of old wheels, a board placed on the axle for a seat, and another board attached by rope for their feet (52). When they arrived safely in the north, Harriet bought them a house in Auburn, New York (80). In December 1860, just before the outbreak of the Civil War, she made her last successful trip to Maryland (83).

As Harriet became more well-known and the bounty on her head increased, her friends begged her to discontinue her dangerous trips. On one occasion, perhaps somewhat exasperated with them, she replied,

> Now look here! John [in the book of Revelation] saw the city, didn't he? Yes, John saw the city. Well, what did he see? He saw twelve gates—three of those gates was on the north—three of them was

on the east—and three of them was on the west—but there was three of them on the South too; and I reckon if they kill me down there, I'll get into one of them gates, don't you? (36)

She made clear again and again that she faced only two choices: "There's two things I've got a right to, and these are, Death or Liberty—one or t'other I mean to have. No one will take me back alive; I shall fight for my liberty, and when the time has come for me to go, the Lord will let them kill me" (21). What she claimed for herself—death or liberty—she also claimed for all those she led out of slavery and into freedom.

Throughout her life, her faith in God's provision was unshakable. Once she came to the office of an abolitionist friend and asked for twenty dollars to fund her next rescue trip. "Twenty dollars?" he exclaimed. "Who told you to come here for twenty dollars?"

"The Lord told me, sir."

"Well, I guess the Lord's mistaken this time."

"I guess he isn't sir. Anyhow I going to sit here till I get it."

And she did. Throughout the day she sat and drifted in and out of sleep as people came and went. At the end of the day, when she awoke, she found herself "the happy possessor of sixty dollars, which had been raised among those who came into the office. She went on her way rejoicing" (110).

Another time, as she recounted the story of her last rescue journey, she told of waiting all night behind a tree during a fierce snowstorm that had delayed the fugitives she was to meet. A listener asked, "didn't you almost feel when you were lying alone, as if there was no God," to which Harriet promptly replied, "Oh, no! . . . I just asked Jesus to take care of me, and He never let me get frost-bitten one bit."[15]

In 1868 when Sarah Bradford was preparing to publish *Scenes in the Life of Harriet Tubman*, Frederick Douglass wrote a letter of commendation to Harriet:

> You ask for what you do not need when you call upon me for a word of commendation. I need such words from you far more than you can need them from me, especially where your superior labors and devotion to the cause of the lately enslaved of our land are known as I know them. The difference between us is very marked. Most that I have done and suffered in the service of our cause has been in public, and I have received much encouragement at every step of the way. You on the other hand have labored in a private

---

15. Bradford, *Harriet, The Moses of Her People*, 91.

way. I have wrought in the day—you in the night. I have had the applause of the crowd and the satisfaction that comes of being approved by the multitude, while the most that you have done has been witnessed by a few trembling, scarred, and foot-sore bondmen and women, whom you have led out of the house of bondage, and whose heartfelt "God bless you" has been your only reward. The midnight sky and the silent stars have been the witnesses of your devotion to freedom and of your heroism. (7)

The heroism of Sojourner Truth and Harriet Tubman is undeniable. Their faith and courage gained the respect of African American and white abolitionists and the enslaved people they aided. But they recognized themselves as those who simply listened to and obeyed the voice of God. They were Holy Women, whom God used to help break the power of the slave regime.

8

The Holy Women Fight for Freedom

Look there above the center, where the flag is waving bright;
We are going out of slavery, we are bound for freedom's light;
We mean to show Jeff Davis how the Africans can fight,
  As we go marching on.

—ATTRIBUTED TO SOJOURNER TRUTH[1]

HARRIET TUBMAN'S FAITH WAS known to be truly great, but she shocked the Rev. Henry Highland Garnett during a visit to his home when she had a vision one night of the emancipation of their people. She came down to breakfast singing: "My people are free! My people are free!" Her host was not convinced: "Oh, Harriet! Harriet!" he said. "You've come to torment us before the time; do cease this noise! My grandchildren may see the day of the emancipation of our people, but you and I will never see it." Harriet was undeterred: "I tell you, sir, you'll see it, and you'll see it soon. My people are free! My people are free." When the Emancipation Proclamation was read out on January 1, 1863, Harriet reminded everyone of her prophecy: "I had my jubilee three years ago. I rejoiced all I could then; I can't rejoice no more."[2]

1. Painter, *Sojourner Truth*, 183.
2. Bradford, *Harriet, The Moses of Her People*, 92–93.

The State of Affairs

Considering the enormous wealth and power of the slave regime that existed in the 1850s, few would have blamed Rev. Garnett for doubting Harriet's confident premonition. At the time of Harriet's vision she had already freed many people and now lived as a free woman in Auburn, New York, although she continued to lead raids into Maryland. But Southern elites controlled the three branches of the federal government, and the root of their power was the nearly four million slaves they owned. Laws against the abolitionist movement and the increased power of the slave regime seemed impregnable and emancipation impossible. In 1850, the Fugitive Slave Act was passed to stop abolitionist support of fugitive slaves like Douglass and the Holy Women and the thousand other slaves escaping to freedom each year. The law undermined the missions of the Holy Women by giving slave owners more authority to pursue their human property and to offer financial rewards to citizens and communities who captured and returned escaping slaves. The law even forced white citizens in the North to assist in the recovery of escaped slaves, although many disobeyed it.[3]

Seven years later, the 1857 Dred Scott decision directly challenged Harriet Tubman's attempts to help the enslaved become free by moving them to free states. Scott, an enslaved man, and his family were taken to a free state by his owner. When the Scotts returned to Missouri, Dred and his wife Harriet petitioned for their freedom, although Harriet's case was later dropped. In 1850, the Missouri state court declared Scott free, but that decision was reversed by the State Supreme Court two years later. A district federal court again declared Scott free, but the case then wended its way to the US Supreme Court. Chief Justice Robert Brooke Taney wrote the majority opinion, which was announced in March 1857. It declared three things: 1) that mere residence in a free state did not entitle an enslaved person to his or her freedom; 2) that African Americans could never be citizens of the United States; and 3) that the 1820 Missouri Compromise which had made western and Northern territories free was unconstitutional. Although federal law was now aligned against both individual and national emancipation, many citizens and even states refused to obey this unjust ruling. The case itself helped to propel Abraham Lincoln into the presidency and to rally the Republican party to oppose slavery and its expansion into the new territories.

3. See chapter 7.

The Holy Women Fight for Freedom

In 1858, Harriet Tubman met the abolitionist leader John Brown, whose anti-slavery allies had recently elected a free-state legislature in the Kansas Territory. Brown himself had led armed skirmishes in Kansas against pro-slavery settlers from neighboring Missouri, including the massacre of five men at Pottawatomie Creek in May 1856, which made him a wanted man. Brown anchored his abolitionist beliefs in his Christian faith and was convinced that only the violent overthrow of the slave regime would bring freedom to the millions of enslaved Americans. With Kansas moving toward entering the Union as a free state, which it did in 1861, Brown turned his attention to planning an overthrow of the premier slave state, Virginia.

Brown settled his family in North Elba, New York, a predominantly Black community, and then traveled to Chatham, Ontario in 1858 to convene a constitutional convention that established a governmental structure for the new state he hoped to form. It was in Chatham, where a third of the residents were former fugitive slaves, that Brown met Tubman, who helped him recruit men for his revolutionary army. Frederick Douglass, who agreed that war would probably be necessary to end slavery, did not support Brown's plan to violently attack slaveholders in Virginia. He attempted to dissuade Brown and discouraged Black men from joining his army. But Tubman, whom Brown called "General Tubman" and "one of the best and bravest persons on this continent," had no such qualms.[4] She gathered former slaves now living in Ontario to join his expeditionary force, although in the end Brown attacked Harpers Ferry with only a handful of allies. The raid went badly. Two of Brown's sons, Watson and Oliver, were killed, along with eight others; five escaped; Brown and seven more were captured and hanged in December 1859.

Despite this dismal result, Tubman remained a staunch supporter of John Brown's goals. She often related a dream she had seen repeatedly before she met him in Canada, of "a wilderness sort of place, all full of rocks and bushes" where a serpent raised its head, "and as it did so, it became the head of an old man with a long white beard, gazing at her wishful like, just as if he was going to speak to me." Then two other younger heads arose, "and as she stood looking at them, and wondering what they could want with her, a great crowd of men rushed in and struck down the younger heads, and then the head of the old man." Although the recurring dream perplexed Tubman, when she met John Brown, "he was the very image of

---

4. Bradford, *Harriet, The Moses of Her People*, 134.

the head she had seen," and when she heard of his death, along with that of his sons, she knew that the dream had been a prophecy.[5] She also suspected that she herself would soon be drawn into a broader conflict.

The Civil War Begins

The election of Abraham Lincoln as president of the United States in 1860 was the signal for Southern slaveholding states to secede from the Union.[6] Seven states created the Confederate Constitution in February 1861 and named Jefferson Davis as provisional president of the Confederacy. They were later joined by four more states, and Davis was elected as the Confederacy's first and only president.

The history of the Civil War is often told as a series of battles, victories, and defeats, which began on April 12, 1861 when South Carolina forces fired on and then captured Fort Sumter. After another Confederate victory at the First Battle of Bull Run in July, Lincoln realized that the United States had entered into a prolonged war. Northern warships secured Port Royal, South Carolina, and the surrounding Sea Islands later in 1861, and for the next four years the outcome of the Civil War seesawed between Union and Confederate advances. In 1862, the Confederacy won the Second Battle of Bull Run and took Harpers Ferry but Union forces captured Shiloh, Tennessee and retained control of Antietam, although with heavy losses. After Antietam, President Lincoln announced the Preliminary Emancipation Proclamation, to take effect on January 1 the following year. In 1863, the Union Army gained control of the entire Mississippi River and split the Confederacy into two parts. It also won at the Battle of Gettysburg, but failed to destroy General Lee's army. Generals Grant and Lee met repeatedly in 1864, a year that also saw General Sherman capture Atlanta. Sherman continued his march through the South in 1865, while Jefferson Davis's insistence that the South be recognized as an independent nation scuttled any notion of peace talks. The war was finally resolved on April 7, 1865 at Appomattox Courthouse, when the South surrendered and the Confederacy was dissolved.

This outline of military advances and defeats, however, does not capture the effect the Civil War had on free and enslaved African Americans.

5. Bradford, *Scenes in the Life*, 82–83.

6. This account of the Civil War follows the outline available from the Library of Congress, "Time Line of the Civil War."

The Holy Women Fight for Freedom

For two hundred years they had prayed, worked, and died for freedom. They understood, in their very bodies, the cost of American prosperity. They also understood the economic and political intertwining of North and South.

The "South" was big, as large as Great Britain, France, Austria, Prussia, and Spain combined. Its four million slaves, valued around three billion dollars, created wealth for the South's eight million white citizens. The enslaved were worth more than all the farm land in the South and three times as much as the construction costs for all existing railroad lines throughout the United States. The enslaved produced two-thirds of the commercially grown cotton in the world and four-fifths of the cotton used by Great Britain's textile industry, about half the value of all US exports. But the South's wealth was also intimately linked with that of the North, where the raw goods of tobacco, sugar, rice, hemp, and cotton were both enjoyed and used to manufacture other products. Southern politicians played an outsized role in the United States government: twelve of the fifteen presidents before Lincoln were either slave owners themselves or the allies of slave owners. The US Congress and Supreme Court were similarly dominated by those whose wealth and influence were in some way dependent upon the slave regime.[7]

As the 1850s drew to a close, Black and white abolitionists feared that slavery might be regaining its hold on the nation. Tubman's biographer briskly summarized 1860 as a time of spineless compromise—"the mad winter . . . when State after State, and politician after politician, went down on their knees to beg the South not to secede."[8] The hunting of fugitive slaves became so intense that Harriet's friends rushed her to Canada for her own safety. She went reluctantly and did not remain there for long.

As war loomed, Frederick Douglass, Tubman, and abolitionists who had supported Lincoln's candidacy hoped that he would swiftly act to end slavery. That he did not do so may not have been a surprise, but it was a bitter blow. A single day without promised freedom was one day too many. Both sides also misjudged the heart and tenacity of African Americans. The South, lulled into thinking that slavery enforced by the whip had induced a loyal passivity, thought the enslaved would join their masters in resisting the Northern aggressors. The North, confident that the war would be short, resisted offers of Black men to enlist in the army, fearing that white soldiers

---

7. The facts in this paragraph come from Levine, *Fall of the House of Dixie*, 1–8. The slave-owning presidents were Washington, Jefferson, Madison, Monroe, Jackson, Tyler, Polk, and Taylor; their allies were Van Buren, Fillmore, Pierce, and Buchanan (8).

8. Bradford, *Scenes in the Life*, 84.

would not serve alongside their Black counterparts and that an integrated army would be a barrier to reunification of the nation.

Both North and South were wrong. African Americans were ready to claim their freedom and self-emancipate. They streamed across borders, bringing their families with them to camp out behind Union lines. They rushed to join the Union Army. Those who could not flee the South began campaigns of resistance, disappearing from the cotton fields, tending their own gardens, refusing to cower before those whom they no longer recognized as masters, or simply walking away from the plantations. In sum, as one historian has noted,

> Slavery collapsed under the pounding of federal troops from the outside and the subversion of plantation-bound black men and women from the inside. By war's end, the old order was in disarray.... Whether in flight from their owners, soldiering in the Union army, protesting unequal pay, or demanding compensation for their labor, black people drew upon their collective experience in negotiating with their old masters to address their new liberators. The revolution of emancipation had begun.[9]

Harriet Tubman's War

Soon after Union forces won their first victory at Port Royal, Harriet Tubman decided to travel to South Carolina to provide support both for the enslaved and also to the Union troops who were stationed there. Governor John Andrew of Massachusetts, who asked if she could "go at a moment's notice," helped arrange her transportation to Beaufort, South Carolina.[10] At first, Tubman worked for the YMCA, distributing supplies to the soldiers. With $200 given to her by the government, she set up a center that enabled the newly freed to earn wages by doing washing, sewing, and baking for the troops.[11] Soon, however, Tubman was also employed as a spy and scout, making use of the skills she had honed while rescuing fugitives from Maryland. A general pass, issued by General David Hunter, testifies to her importance to the Union Army:

---

9. Berlin, *Generations of Captivity*, 259.
10. Bradford, *Harriet, The Moses of Her People*, 93.
11. Larson, *Bound for the Promised Land*, 205.

> Pass the bearer, Harriet Tubman, to Beaufort and back to this place [Port Royal], and wherever she wishes to go; and give her free passage at all times, on all Government transports. Harriet was sent to me from Boston by Governor Andrew, of Massachusetts, and is a valuable woman. She has permission, as a servant of the Government, to purchase such provisions from the Commissary as she may need.[12]

As a veteran supporter of John Brown's raids against the slave states, Tubman was also eager to see free and enslaved Black men enlist in the Union Army. She was joined in this desire by Frederick Douglass, who presciently prophesied that fighting for Union would be the first step toward gaining full citizenship for African Americans:

> Once let the black man get upon his person the brass letters US, let him get an eagle on his button, and a musket on his shoulder, and bullets in his pocket, and there is no power on earth or under the earth which can deny that he has earned the right of citizenship in the United States.[13]

Yet the early efforts of African Americans to enlist in the Army were rebuffed, not least by now-President Lincoln, whose desire to preserve the United States was stronger than the pressure to free the enslaved. One of Tubman's Boston friends, Lydia Maria Child, reported that Harriet was frustrated with Lincoln and told her in conversation that "God's ahead of master Lincoln. God won't let master Lincoln beat the South till he does *the right thing*. . . . He can do it by setting the negroes free."[14]

Lincoln's new government also issued no definitive statement on the treatment of fugitive slaves. General Benjamin Butler in Virginia gave refuge to the enslaved who had been forced to work for the Confederacy, declaring that they were "contraband of war," a label that stuck to them for the duration of the conflict. Butler also set them to work for the Union, although they were not always paid for their labor. However, a few months later, when the general moved to Louisiana, he ordered fugitive slaves to be returned to their owners. Fellow Generals Halleck and Scott favored and enforced this policy of returning fugitives. On the other hand, General Sumner and other abolitionists demanded that the government issue a clear

---

12. Bradford, *Harriet, The Moses of Her People*, 140.

13. Douglass, *Douglass' Monthly* 5 (August 1863), 852; quoted in Chicago History Museum, "New Birth of Freedom."

14. As quoted in Larson, *Bound for the Promised Land*, 206.

policy to protect fugitives and guarantee emancipation.[15] Finally, in August 1861, Congress declared all fugitive slaves to be free, although it did not set aside funds to support and employ them. The following year, General Rufus Saxton, the military governor of the Department of the South, which oversaw abandoned plantations, ordered that newly freed families were to be given two acres for each "working hand" in the family, with tools supplied by the government. They were expected to produce food for themselves, as well as a certain amount of cotton for government use.[16]

A year later, General Saxton was finally given permission under the newly passed Militia Act to recruit five thousand African Americans into the Union Army. He reactivated the First South Carolina Volunteer Regiment, which had been recruited and dismissed a few months earlier, and trained them in Port Royal under the command of Colonel Thomas Wentworth Higginson. On January 1, 1863, the Emancipation Proclamation ended the ambiguity over the enlistment of African Americans: it ordered that all people "declared to be free" and "of suitable condition, will be received into the armed service of the United States." Frederick Douglass's sons, Louis and Charles, enlisted in the 54th Massachusetts Infantry, as did Sojourner Truth's grandson, James Caldwell. Eventually some 166 Black regiments were formed and over two hundred thousand men, one-tenth of the entire Union Army, actively participated in the war, although they remained in segregated units and often received less pay than their white counterparts. More than thirty-eight thousand died.[17] Nevertheless, their service as soldiers, along with the support provided by thousands of African American civilian workers, was crucial to winning the war.

Although both Black and white abolitionists celebrated the Emancipation Proclamation of 1863, they understood that it did not unambiguously guarantee the freedom, dignity, and equality of African Americans. Black soldiers were not automatically granted the same pay as their white counterparts, and they usually served under white command. Fugitives found few means of support once they left the plantations. Black workers were not welcomed in cities, where jobs were scarce. Nor were all the enslaved freed. Slavery remained legal in the border states of Maryland, Delaware, Kentucky, and Missouri, which had not seceded from the Union. Tennessee and portions of Virginia and Louisiana that were now under the

---

15. Franklin, *From Slavery to Freedom*, 272–73.
16. Franklin, *From Slavery to Freedom*, 274.
17. Franklin, *From Slavery to Freedom*, 293.

control of the Union Army were also exempted. Although the defeat of the Confederacy in April 1865 meant the end of slavery in the United States, the enslaved in Galveston, Texas were not informed of their freedom until June 19, a day now celebrated as the Juneteenth federal holiday. Enslaved persons were not legally freed until the 13th Amendment, passed by Congress in January 1865, was ratified on December 6, 1865.[18]

While some praised President Lincoln for issuing the Proclamation and others excoriated him, many African Americans saw it merely as one means that God was using to answer their long prayers. As Pastor J. W. C. Pennington, a well-known Black abolitionist and ordained Congregational minister, said in a speech on August 24, 1863, "We should remember that emancipation was resorted to, as a purely military necessity imposed upon this Government in the Providence of an alwise God. The President has no alternative but to fall into the powerful current of events which God had put in motion."[19] Although he had been a committed pacifist before the war, Pennington now encouraged his fellow African Americans to fight, even if "we may have to face, in the field, an army of our own colored brethren of the South," armed by the Confederacy.[20] Although Pennington's fears of a large enslaved army proved unfounded, despite a bill passed in 1865 by the Confederacy authorizing their recruitment, his challenge to Black troops rang in their ears and hearts:

> On our side, the only wise and safe course is to press rapidly into the heart of the slave country, and work out the problem of the Proclamation of freedom. We must prove to the slaves that we have both the will and the power to give effect to the proclamation, and that it is not a mere sound, reaching their ears, upon the wings of the wind.[21]

Harriet Tubman indeed had both "the will and the power to give effect to the proclamation." She was already in South Carolina when the First South Carolina Regiment was formed. Her most famous exploit, however, took place with the Second South Carolina Infantry, commanded by Colonel James Montgomery, who had also served under John Brown. In June 1863, Colonel Higginson asked Tubman to accompany Montgomery as a guide along the Combahee River. The Union gunboats, under Montgomery

---

18. Mississippi, the last state to ratify the 13th Amendment, did so in 2013.
19. Pennington, "Position and Duties," 404.
20. Pennington, "Position and Duties," 404.
21. Pennington, "Position and Duties," 405.

Faith Confronts Evil

and Tubman's direction, were tasked with removing Confederate torpedoes from the river, cutting off supply lines to the rebels, and destroying the plantations. As they passed by the plantations, word spread among the enslaved that the boats were "Lincoln's gun-boats come to set them free" and people began rushing down to the river, carrying whatever they could grab in an instant.[22] Harriet commanded the rescue efforts and, when the fugitives threatened to swamp the small boats that would carry them to the gunboats in the middle of the river, began to encourage the terrified enslaved by singing:

> Of all the whole creation in the East or in the West,
> The glorious Yankee nation is the greatest and the best.
> Come along! Come along! Don't be alarmed,
> Uncle Sam is rich enough to give you all a farm.[23]

Eventually, her biographer wrote, "they were all brought on board. The masters fled; houses and barns and railroad bridges were burned, tracks torn up, torpedoes destroyed, and the object of the expedition was fully accomplished."[24]

Later Harriet wrote "Don't you think we colored people are entitled to some credit for that exploit? . . . We weakened the rebels somewhat on the Combahee River, by taking and bringing away seven hundred and fifty-six head of their most valuable live stock, known up in your region as 'contrabands,' and this, too, without the loss of a single life on our part."[25] The "live stock" to whom she refers were, of course, enslaved people, and Tubman apparently used the term deliberately to foreground the inhumanity of their situation.

The Combahee River expedition was a hazardous undertaking, but Tubman also found moments of humor. Recounting her rescue of one small family in a letter to friends in the North she said,

> I was carrying two pigs for a poor sick woman, who had a child to carry, and the order "double quick" was given, and I started to run, stepped on my dress, it being rather long, and fell and tore it almost off, so that when I got on board the boat, there was hardly anything left of it but shreds. I made up my mind then I would

---

22. Bradford, *Harriet, The Moses of Her People*, 100.
23. Bradford, *Harriet, The Moses of Her People*, 102.
24. Bradford, *Harriet, The Moses of Her People*, 102.
25. Bradford, *Scenes in the Life*, 86.

never wear a long dress on another expedition of the kind, but would have a bloomer as soon as I could get it.[26]

She then added this request: "I want, among the rest, a bloomer dress, made of some coarse, strong material, to wear on expeditions.... So please make this known to the ladies, if you will, for I expect to have use for it very soon, probably before they can get it to me."[27]

In addition to her active roles on the front line, Harriet also nursed the soldiers in the field hospitals, often using her knowledge of roots and herbs to stem the smallpox, dysentery, malaria, and other fevers that threatened to claim many lives. Harriet gave this account of her labors in the hospital:

> I'd go to the hospital, I would, early every morning. I'd get a big chunk of ice, I would, and put it in a basin, and fill it with water: then I'd take a sponge and begin. First man I'd come to, I'd thrash away the flies, and they'd rise, they would, like bees round a hive. Then I'd begin to bathe their wounds, and by the time I'd bathed off three or four, the fire and heat would have melted the ice and made the water warm, and it would be as red as clear blood. Then I'd go and get more ice, I would, and by the time I got to the next ones, the flies would be round the first ones black and thick as ever.[28]

Despite this crucial labor, Harriet was not paid for her services. At night she would make pies, gingerbread, and root beer, which someone would sell for her the next day to provide enough money to sustain herself and others whom she helped.

Tubman was not the only heroic African American woman to work on behalf of the Union. Susie King Taylor, who also served with the First South Carolina Volunteer Regiment as cook, laundress, and reading instructor, recorded that

> there were hundreds of [African American women] who assisted the Union soldiers by hiding them and helping them to escape. Many were punished for taking food to the prison stockades for the prisoners.... The soldiers were starving, and these women did all they could towards relieving those men, although they knew the penalty, should they be caught giving them aid. Others assisted in various ways the Union army. These things should be kept in history before the people. There has never been a greater war in

---

26. Bradford, *Scenes in the Life*, 86.
27. Bradford, *Scenes in the Life*, 85–86.
28. Bradford, *Harriet, The Moses of Her People*, 97.

the United States than the one of 1861, where so many lives were lost,—not men alone but noble women as well.[29]

Many other women engineered emancipation for themselves and their families. The Miller brothers were soldiers in Colonel Higginson's regiment. Their grandparents, enslaved on a plantation near Savannah, were seized after a failed escape attempt and the grandfather was sentenced to five hundred lashes. As Higginson recounted the story,

> while the white men on the plantation were viewing the punishment, [the grandmother] was collecting her children and grandchildren, to the number of twenty-two, in a neighboring marsh, preparatory to another attempt that night. They found a flat-boat which had been rejected as unseaworthy, got on board, —still under the old woman's orders, —and drifted forty miles down the river to our lines. . . . When the "flat" touched the side of the [Union gunboat], the grandmother rose to her full height, with her youngest grandchild in her arms, and said only, "My God! are we free?" By one of those coincidences of which life is full, her husband escaped also, after his punishment, and was taken up by the same gunboat.[30]

Although the colonel may have considered it a "coincidence," the Miller family undoubtedly saw the hand of God in the rescue and preservation of their family.

These women's steadfast courage and service contrasted with the ambivalence of the Union's commander-in-chief. Tubman and other abolitionists chafed under Lincoln's reluctance to end slavery, his initial refusal to allow Blacks to fight for the Union, and his plan, formalized in Section 11 of the District of Columbia Emancipation Act of 1862, to use $100,000 "to aid in the colonization and settlement of such free persons of African descent now residing in said District . . . to emigrate to the Republic of Hayti or Liberia, or such other country beyond the limits of the United States as the President may determine."[31] For those who had been fighting for their freedom as Americans, this reversion to a scheme for colonization that had been previously rejected was deeply troubling.[32]

---

29. Taylor, *Reminiscences of My Life*, 67–68.
30. Higginson, *Army Life*, 247.
31. An Act of April 16, 1862.
32. See chapter 4.

Sojourner Truth's War

Shortly after the Emancipation Proclamation reversed governmental policy and called for Black men to join the military, the First Michigan Colored Infantry Regiment, which later became the 102nd US Colored Infantry, began to recruit volunteers. In November 1863, Sojourner Truth organized a Thanksgiving Day dinner for the troops from Battle Creek, where she was now living, who were training at Camp Ward in Detroit. She not only collected donations and delivered the food herself, but also cheered the troops with "a speech glowing with patriotism, exhortation, and good wishes" and spent time talking with the young soldiers "in motherly conversation."[33] It is reported that later she composed a song, to the tune of "The Battle Hymn of the Republic," to encourage the young men:

> Look there above the center, where the flag is waving bright;
> We are going out of slavery, we are bound for freedom's light;
> We mean to show Jeff Davis how the Africans can fight,
>   As we go marching on.
>
> Father Abraham has spoken, and the message has been sent;
> The prison doors have opened, and out the prisoners went
> To join the sable army of African descent,
>   As we go marching on.[34]

The following spring, Sojourner set off on a lecture tour of New York before traveling down to Washington to see President Lincoln. She reported that she was received graciously by Lincoln, and when she told him that she "had never heard of him before he was talked of for president, he smilingly replied, 'I had heard of you many times before that'" (178). Sojourner used her time in Washington to speak and raise funds for the Colored Soldiers' Aid Society (177), but soon discovered that more was needed, particularly at Freedman's Village in Arlington, Virginia, a refugee camp located on the plantation that had belonged to Robert E. Lee, where many of the formerly enslaved had been sent to create a new life for themselves. "I think I can be useful and will stay," she told her friends (179). In December 1864, she received official status for her work at the village. Her commission read:

---

33. Truth, *Narrative of Sojourner Truth*, 173. Subsequent page numbers in this section refer to the *Narrative*; speeches written in dialect are transcribed.

34. Painter, *Sojourner Truth*, 183–84.

> This certifies that The National Freedman's Relief Association has appointed Sojourner Truth to be a counselor to the freed people at Arlington Heights, Va., and hereby commends her to the favor and confidence of the officers of government, and of all persons who take an interest in relieving the condition of the freedmen, or in promoting their intellectual, moral, and religious instruction. (181–82)

In the year that Sojourner spent at Freedman's Village, she did more than promote instruction. When residents of Maryland, a slave state that had not joined the Confederacy but was not fully committed to the Union, took children from the village as their "servants," she told the grieving parents that this was an outrage. She told them "that they were free, and had rights which would be recognized and maintained by the laws, and that they could bring these robbers to justice" (182–83). When the Marylanders threatened to put her in jail, she told them that at the first attempt to do so, she "would make the United States rock like a cradle" (183). By September 1865, she was commissioned to serve in the Freedman's Hospital and the chief surgeon was ordered to provide "all facilities and authority" she needed (183).

While her work at Freedman's Village was honored, Sojourner herself had to contend with the racist culture that permeated Washington, DC and its surrounding states. She was instrumental in eliminating the "Jim Crow" car from the streetcar system, but she was repeatedly ignored or harassed when she tried to board the now integrated system and take her seat. On at least one occasion, she told the conductor that she didn't fear his threats, since she was "from the Empire State of New York, and knew the laws as well as he did" (185). When another conductor threatened to throw her off the car, she responded, "If you attempt that, it will cost you more than your car and horses are worth" (185). Eventually a conductor threw her against a door as he tried to evict her, injured her shoulder, and lost the lawsuit she and the Freedman's Bureau brought against him. Sojourner was jubilant and reported: "before the trial was ended, the inside of the cars looked like pepper and salt. . . . Now they who had so lately cursed me for wanting to ride, could stop for black as well as white, and could even condescend to say, 'Walk in ladies'" (187).

After the War

Shortly after the war ended, in July 1865, Harriet Tubman was appointed "nurse or matron at the Colored Hospital, Fort Monroe, Virginia."[35] Unfortunately, the generosity of Uncle Sam, which she had praised in song as the enslaved rushed toward the Northern gunboats on the Combahee River, failed to materialize. She was denied a permanent position and soon returned to Auburn, New York where her elderly parents and other dependents lived. She struggled in the following years to support them and retain her property. Her friends petitioned for her to receive a pension. General Saxton wrote that he could "bear witness to the value of her services in South Carolina and Florida. She was employed in the hospitals and as a spy. She made many a raid inside the enemy's lines, displaying remarkable courage, zeal, and fidelity... and is as deserving of a pension from the Government for her services as any other of its faithful servants."[36] Yet the small pension she eventually received came not from her service to the Union but as compensation after her husband, also a veteran, died.

Nor did Tubman receive a modicum of respect from those who did not know, or care to know, of her heroic exploits. Traveling on a train through New Jersey on her way back to New York, a white conductor "thrust her out of the car with such violence that she has not been able to work scarcely any since."[37] The stories of African American veterans being forcibly evicted from streetcars, busses, and trains, told here by Sojourner Truth and Harriet Tubman, are repeated with mind-numbing regularity. Susie King Taylor, whose husband had also served with the First South Carolina Volunteer Regiment, recalled being denied access to a suitable train carriage as she traveled to Louisiana in 1898 to nurse her desperately ill son. When she could not procure a sleeper to bring him home to Boston, she wrote that "I was forced to let him remain where he was. It seemed very hard, when his father fought to protect the Union and our flag, and yet his boy was denied, under this same flag, a berth to carry him home to die, because he was a negro."[38]

In her later years, Harriet Tubman continued to support her extended family and her AME Zion Church in Auburn. She was active in the suffrage movement, and was a featured speaker at the first meeting of the

---

35. Bradford, *Harriet, The Moses of Her People*, 142.
36. Bradford, *Harriet, The Moses of Her People*, 142.
37. Bradford, *Scenes in the Life*, 24.
38. Taylor, *Reminiscences of My Life*, 71–72.

National Association of Colored Women in 1896, which was formed in response to the increasing racism in the National American Woman Suffrage Association.[39]

Sojourner Truth continued after the war to help the former enslaved find their footing in the North. In 1867, she made three trips to bring workers from the South to New York, where they might find jobs and new homes. But she soon recognized that although the Civil War had officially ended slavery in the reunited United States, many of the enslaved had merely been transmuted into refugees in the nation's capital. They had, as her biographer noted, "no possessions but the bodies which had recently been given them by a dash of Abraham Lincoln's pen."[40] Government aid was insufficient; private resources had to be constantly solicited; racism, of the kind Truth, Tubman, and Taylor encountered on streetcars and trains, as well as other acts of violence, was daily endured. Many of the newly freed were still treated as less than human. They had indeed become a commodity, the "contraband" that the Union Army had named them.

Susie King Taylor spoke for many when she wrote in 1902:

> I wonder if our white fellow men realize the true sense of meaning of brotherhood? For two hundred years we had toiled for them; the war of 1861 came and was ended, and we thought our race was forever freed from bondage, and that the two races could live in unity with each other, but when we read almost every day of what is being done to my race by some whites in the South, I sometimes ask, "Was the war in vain? Has it brought freedom, in the full sense of the word, or has it not made our condition more hopeless?"... Justice we ask,—to be citizens of these United States, where so many of our people have shed their blood with their white comrades, that the stars and stripes should never be polluted.[41]

Sojourner Truth was one of those who continued to press for justice after the war. She remained in Washington, DC, determined to bring reparations to the formerly enslaved. "*We helped* to pay this cost," she said.

> We have been a source of wealth to this republic. Our labor supplied the country with cotton, until villages and cities dotted the enterprising North for its manufacture, and furnished employment

---

39. Larson, *Bound for the Promised Land*, 275.

40. Truth, *Narrative of Sojourner Truth*, 192. Subsequent page numbers in this section refer to the *Narrative*; speeches written in dialect are transcribed.

41. Taylor, *Reminiscences of My Life*, 61–62; 75–76.

The Holy Women Fight for Freedom

and support for a multitude, thereby becoming a revenue to the government. Beneath a burning southern sun have we toiled, in the canebrake and the rice swamp, urged on by the merciless driver's lash, earning millions of money; and so highly were we valued there, that should one poor wretch venture to escape from this hell of slavery, no exertion of man or trained blood-hound was spared to seize and return him to his field of unrequited labor.... Our nerves and sinews, our tears and blood, have been sacrificed on the altar of this nation's avarice. Our unpaid labor has been a stepping-stone to its financial success. Some of its dividends must surely be ours. (196–97)

Sojourner did not merely advocate for reparations. She provided a practical plan. She petitioned Congress to set aside public lands and provide the financial and educational resources for the recently enslaved to create a new, self-sufficient life for themselves in the West, away from the deadly refugee camp that Washington, DC had become. If Congress could give land to the railroads and their wealthy owners, she reasoned, it could give land to those who had worked so long without payment. "You owe it to them," she said, "because you took away from them all they earned and made them what they are.... You are the cause of the brutality of these poor creatures. For you're the children of those who enslaved them" (226). In support of this plan, she embarked on lecture tours, solicited additional signatures, raised funds, and threw herself into the effort to make it a reality. At the same time, she resisted, as many had before her, the renewed suggestions that free Black people should be resettled in Liberia (239).

Sojourner Truth grew increasingly frustrated at having her speeches well-received, but without the forthcoming political and financial support that was needed to realize her western dream. "Everybody says this is a good work," she complained, "but nobody helps" (240). She became an even more committed feminist, convinced that if women were able to exercise political power, everyone would be better served. "Did Jesus ever say anything against women?" she would ask. "Not a word. But he did speak awful hard things against the men. You know what they were. And he knew them to be true. But he didn't say nothing against the women" (220). A Battle Creek newspaper reported that she told them, "If ever the Augean stables of our political temple are to be cleared, it must be done by woman, and that it never will be clean until she is admitted to full fellowship therein" (230). Shortly before the election of General Grant as president, she went to the third ward in Battle Creek and demanded to have her name listed as a registered voter. She was refused. She returned on the day of the election with the same demand. She was again refused, but the *Battle Creek Journal* reported that she was determined "to continue the assertion of her right, until she gains it" (232).

Although Sojourner Truth did not gain the right to vote during her lifetime, she continued to be active in the suffrage movement, as well as in various plans to resettle formerly enslaved persons in the West.

Epilogue

Before, during, and after the Civil War, African Americans believed that God would destroy the slave regime. They prayed and worked to that end, and even when they seemed most oppressed, they testified to their faith in an all-powerful God. Told by her owners that the Union Army had been defeated, Fannie Dawson, a young houseslave, replied:

> Ain't God the captain? He started this war, and He's right in front. He may stop in his career and let you rest up a little bit now, but our Captain ain't never been beaten. Soon He'll start out again, and you'll hear the bugle blow, and He'll march on to victory. . . . For I'm as certain this war will set us free as that I stand here.[42]

Fannie Dawson was right, and she echoed the words of many African American prayer warriors who could now rejoice in the emancipation of nearly four million slaves, just as Harriet Tubman had predicted. In 1833, Maria Stewart had described the slave regime as a modern-day Babylon. In April 1865, when the all-Black Twenty-Fifth Corps of the United States Colored Troops marched through Richmond to accept its formal surrender, they heard cheers and songs: "Babylon is fallen, Babylon is fallen. I'm going to occupy the land." Spectators called out to the Black soldiers, "God bless you!" and "Jesus has opened the way!"[43]

In the end, the Civil War's winners were neither Union generals or soldiers, but the freed people whose faith hastened the slave regime's end. Although the former slaves did not gain the "forty acres and a mule" they had been promised, the newly freed people began their own reconstruction. Among the ruins of former plantations, they built house churches that doubled as schools where they could freely pursue their desire to learn and

---

42. Ward, *Slaves' War*, 102.
43. Levine, *Fall of the House of Dixie*, 273.

worship. Though they had to struggle for a share of political power, the Union victory and slave regime's destruction restored their humanity. They now had the freedom to marry and start families and communities of their own.

For nearly three hundred years, African American women from the Birthmothers to the Holy Women had experienced the full range of slavery in the United States. In early America, they had been owned by presidents who were wealthy planters. Yet they were freed by a president who owned neither slave nor plantation. The Lord came to two illiterate enslaved Holy Women and anointed them with truth and courage to spiritually guide the dismantling of an evil regime that held their people in bondage for generations. The Holy Women's legacy to future generations of Christian believers was their faith and commitment to the spiritual weapons of biblical truth, worship, and prayer to move the hand of God.

Afterword

The Work of Hope

BARBARA OMOLADE AND SUSAN Felch materialize hope in difficult places. This is no small gift of the Spirit. There are not enough people who know how to do this today. Many of the students I teach do not know what it means to hope. But let me quickly add that there is nothing wrong with them. I understand this inability to hope—we could even call this a loss of hope—to be in fact the exhaustion of a kind of hope. The kind of hope that does not have deep roots in a practice of faith that is at the same time an intellectual practice.

The first time I met Barbara Omolade, I knew I was in the presence of a woman who articulated a practice of faith that was an intellectual practice. This would not be an unusual or even a commendable thing in and of itself, because there are people whose faith and intellect are woven together in terribly harmful ways and turned toward enacting oppression. But Barbara Omolade enacts a faith and an intellectual practice with deep roots in Black Christian life. It is a faith that she has come to understand so well. Indeed, she saw *in the faith* of Black people, especially Black women, an intellectual practice that needed to be considered more carefully by those who should have eyes to see but for a myriad of reasons did not see. Of course, one could call Barbara a womanist thinker and that would be correct. She shares the same sensibilities so powerfully seen in the founding mothers of womanist theology and ethics, like Katie Geneva Cannon and Diana L. Hayes. Yet Barbara Omolade journeyed in a different world than the world of theological studies.

Barbara throughout her career has been able to see the workings of Black women, the-one-step-forward-two-steps-back, the struggles and the victories, the signifying, the creating, the dreaming, and with precision, the thinking, always the thinking. Barbara, the Christian who is a

Afterword

Black feminist, the Black feminist who is a Christian, has always embodied a faith that refuses constriction, shuns boundaries, and demands a new kind of serious attention to the words and wisdom of Black women. This is Barbara's rising song—Can you hear the sound of Black Christian women thinking their faith amid mind-bending oppression? Barbara can hear and invites shared hearing.

This hearing is urgently needed now, as so many people are walking away from Christianity. The walking away is necessary given the kind of Christianity that so many Christians in the Western world inherited through the legacies of modern colonialism. That was and is a Christianity bound up in the control of bodies and places. Controlling the bodies of women, especially women of color, was always a feverish preoccupation of missionary colonial powers. The logic behind that control was diabolically forward thinking—to control the future, it would be necessary to control (enslave) the means of production, of future slaves, of productive life, and of expanding profit. That control aligned nicely with a particular way of understanding what salvation should look like embodied in indigenous peoples by making them the mirror image of white Europeans.

This history is not the only reason so many are walking away from Christianity. Many are walking away because this history still moves forward in the forms of white supremacy and patriarchy that continue to render Black life as the fuel to be burned for white Western life to flourish. When so many people, especially students, look at the Christianity around them, the one deeply wedded to white supremacy and white privilege, the one committed to the control of bodies, the one that glories in capitalist exploitation of the planet and all life, they recoil even if they were raised in such a Christianity.

If the walking away is necessary, what are they walking toward? This is the question that confronts all Christian institutions today. There can be no going back, but to move forward there must be a recalibration of the path we are on. That recalibration means looking back at a Christianity that formed inside deformed colonial Christianity.

Black Christianity was and is a complex form of faith. Never immune to the colonial wounding of Western Christianity, it has always been much more than those wounds. Yet it takes intellectual and spiritual patience to see it beyond its wounds and its wounding. Indeed, there are sectors of Black Christianity that align so tightly with colonial Christianity that it is very difficult to see any substantial difference and therefore any reason not to join the

Afterword

exodus away from it. There is, however, reason not to leave Christian faith, and Barbara offers it to readers in this text as she tells stories familiar to many but not to everyone and understood by some people but not by enough. In this regard, Omolade has stepped into an old debate with fresh insight.

That old debate is over how we should read Christian agency for Black slaves and ex-slaves during the ante- and postbellum periods. Some have argued that too much of the master class thinks itself through the slaves to place too much stock on their pronouncements and their ways of thinking. Others glory in the Christian confession of Black slaves and their children while turning slavery itself into a minor matter in the overarching victory of faith. Still others have largely ignored the actual thinking of these chained saints, preferring to focus on the conditions of their enslavement—the social, political, economic, gendered, and human subject forming machinations of the enslaving operations and noting the responses of the enslaved at the level of gauging their reactions to these macro forces and their micro effects.

Omolade strives for a better path. She keeps sight of the conditions of slavery and white supremacy but shows the Black thinking subject in prayer and protest, in praise and planning, in spiritual striving and strategic cunning. This is where thinking the faith must begin—where people are confronting a Christianity that denies its own freedom, a Christianity married to whiteness. There are not enough Christian scholars, whether they be pastors, or professors, or writers, or artists, who are engaged in this confrontation and therefore not enough who are offering those in exodus from Christianity a path forward into a better faith, a hopeful faith. Barbara's powerful journey prepared her to write a path forward for us and it also prepared her to meet Susan Felch. To be in their presence was to be in the presence of not only a beautiful friendship, but a shared journey of making sense of a faith-filled intellectual life that stood against white male Christian hegemony.

Anyone who has read Susan Felch's work and listened to her think out loud would repeat the famous slogan that Robert D. Richardson used for his book on Emerson—this is a mind on fire. Not only a beautiful writer, but a clear-eyed interpreter of texts and life, Susan was the perfect intellectual collaborator for Barbara. Together they dreamed the what-if—what if the lives of those Christians at the margin were taken seriously as sites for thinking the faith? Susan knows a bit of that marginality herself. Raised in that sometimes lovely adjacency that comes with being a white missionary kid born and/or raised outside of North American white culture. There is a

Afterword

saving grace in being an outsider especially when people mistake you for an insider. Watching Barbara and Susan operate inside North American white Christian culture as it manifested itself at Calvin College (now University) was always a joy, because they saw what others often could not or would not see. They saw problems of course, but they also saw possibilities.

The goal of Christian intellectual life is to see the problems all the way to their roots, but also to see the possibilities all the way into the life of God, indeed our life with God. Barbara and Susan saw both clearly. It takes skill to see, as Barbara did in this book, Christian striving turned against slaveholding Christianity. It takes even more skill to write in such a way that students just beginning their scholarly journey may see that striving and possibly mark their own striving alongside that of these former slaves, their spiritual ancestors.

There are many Christian scholars in this world and especially the Western world who refuse any serious consideration of Black slave life, or slavery, or Black Christian life past or present, choosing instead to abide in a vision of their faith that avoids deep reflection on the problem of whiteness and the fear so many feel when the idea of whiteness is mentioned. That refusal is on massive display in our time, with many white Christians leading the charge against any educational inquiry into the Western world's slave past or its white supremacist present. They would prefer to see blindly their Christianity as in need of protection and see their own lives under attack for simply being white. Such resistance is founded on a lie born of a diseased Christianity. The lie is that whiteness is a God-given reality of creation, that racial existence speaks of a created order, that white supremacy is not real, and that our current social order first needs defending because Christianity and Christian faith is deeply woven into it. This diseased Christianity, following in the patterns of slaveholding Christianity, resists its own healing and deliverance. It cannot find its way out of captivity without the help of nonwhite Christians who have sought and yet seek their authentic freedom in Jesus Christ. My word to them and to the many students who I hope will find their way to this book is this—Herein you will find Christian striving embodied in Black women and thereby gain a glimpse of your freedom. Pay attention to what Barbara Omolade is saying if you wish to be free and live in the hope of yet more freedom in this world.

Willie James Jennings
Hamden, Connecticut

In Memory of
Dr. Barbara Jones Omolade

October 29, 1942–July 10, 2023

DR. BARBARA J. OMOLADE was born in 1942 at St. John's Hospital in Brooklyn, NY to Hugh Emmanuel and Mamie Taylor Jones. Her father was a veteran of World War II and later an ambulance driver, and her mother was a full-time homemaker; both were avid gardeners. Barbara grew up at 746 Macon Street in Bedford Stuyvesant with her sister Beatrice, attended Bridge Street AME Church, was a stellar pupil at her elementary school, and was chosen as a young preteen to be the first African American student to integrate her middle school. Her parents surrounded her with unconditional love and attention, so that by her own testimony, she never knew a day of hunger or strife. She often took trips in the summer to her mother's hometown in Windsor, North Carolina, where she learned to appreciate her family history. During her junior high school years, she began to read novels and developed a love of learning; she read many books about other people's challenges and struggles. She often attributed her focus on education to her parents, who insisted that she pursue a higher education degree; she graduated from Queens College in 1964.

Throughout her life, Barbara was committed to challenging forces that prohibited people from pursuing a dignified existence. In the 1960s, she joined The Student Nonviolent Coordinating Committee (SNCC). She later worked at The Center for the Elimination of Violence in the Family and the Women's Action Alliance in New York City in the 1970s. In the 1980s, she was a founding member of The Center for Worker Education of the City College of New York and spent the next twenty years in academia. The Center for Worker Education (CWE) was the first bachelor's degree

In Memory of Dr. Barbara Jones Omolade

program for working adults in the City University of New York (CUNY). She created and taught some of the first courses on Black women's history at City College and later introduced courses on Race, Class, and Ethnicity and The Culture of Beauty. Her teaching made it possible for the predominantly Black American and Caribbean American working-class students enrolled at CWE during that era to see themselves in the curriculum. Barbara also extended these important conversations to community contexts. Barbara's scholarly work on the histories and experiences of Black women in the United States was transformative as her theorizations compelled the academy to take seriously the intersection of race, gender, and class.

Barbara was also a founder and co-director of the Consultation of African American Christian Scholars, a weeklong seminar held annually at Calvin University from 2001–2005, under the auspices of the Calvin Center for Christian Scholarship. Barbara was curious and courageous as exemplified by her adventures living on a kibbutz in Israel and touring China with an organization that was building US/Chinese relations, as well as forging a new position as the first Dean for Multicultural Affairs at Calvin College (now University).

Barbara was a devoted and faithful Christian, who gave her life to Christ and was baptized in 1994 at the age of fifty-one. She recalled making the decision to become a Christian with a prayer, "Lord have mercy on me, a sinner." She spent the next thirty years of her life intensely growing in her relationship with God, studying the Bible, and attending various churches in New York and Michigan. She moved to Princess Anne, Maryland in 2009 and made Metropolitan United Methodist Church her home church.

In addition to many essays, Barbara authored *The Rising Song of African American Women* (Routledge, 1994). She was an exemplary scholar and educator and was highly regarded for her work as a sociologist and administrator. During her years of retirement, Barbara continued to read, research, and write, with a special interest in the lives of African American Christian women. She completed *Faith Confronts Evil* just a few weeks before her death. As guiding verses during retirement, she looked to Psalm 118: "I shall not die, but live, and shall declare the works of the Lord. He has chastened me sorely, but He has not given me over to death. I will confess, praise, and give thanks to You for You have heard and answered me and You have become my Salvation and Deliverer."

Her children wrote of her last days: "Our mother was fiercely determined even to the end. Although she needed constant oxygen pumps to breathe and could barely stand and walk, her mind was sharp and intact. She had so many plans and ideas. She lived a full life, leaving us with a legacy of love and wisdom. A week before her passing she said, 'Write this verse down, this sickness is a Lazarus moment, my life is for the glory of God' (John 11:1–4)."

Barbara Omolade is survived by her sister, Beatrice Jones, and her four children: Kip Omolade (Diana), Ngina Mandouma (Ghislain), Eskimo Omolade, and Krishna Omolade and her eight grandchildren: Genese, James, Adison, Jonathan, Kent, Kace, Sky, and Trevor. She is also survived by extended family members and friends whom she loved dearly.

Barbara left family and friends a legacy of wisdom and righteous living. She leaves to all her readers a legacy of faith, a *Faith that Confronts Evil*, and is victorious.

Bibliography

An Act of April 16, 1862 [For the Release of Certain Persons Held to Service or Labor in the District of Columbia]. https://catalog.archives.gov/id/299814?objectPanel=transcription&objectPage=3.

Allen, Richard. *The Life, Experience, and Gospel Labours of the Rt. Rev. Richard Allen.* Philadelphia: Martin & Boden, 1833.

Bassard, Katherine Clay. *Spiritual Interrogations: Culture, Gender, and Community in Early African American Women's Writing.* Princeton: Princeton University Press, 1999.

Berlin, Ira. *Generations of Captivity: A History of African-American Slaves.* Cambridge: Belknap, 2003.

Berry, Henry. *The Speech of Henry Berry (of Jefferson) in the House of Delegates of Virginia, on the Abolition of Slavery.* 1832. https://openlibrary.org/books/OL6526329M/The_speech_of_Henry_Berry.

Blassingame, John W., ed. *Slave Testimony: Two Centuries of Letters, Speeches, Interviews, and Autobiographies.* Baton Rouge: Louisiana State University Press, 1977.

Botkin, Benjamin Albert, ed. *Lay My Burden Down: A Folk History of Slavery.* Chicago: University of Chicago Press, 1945.

Bradford, Sarah H. *Harriet, The Moses of Her People.* New York: Geo. R. Lockwood & Son, 1886.

———. *Scenes in the Life of Harriet Tubman.* Auburn, NY: W. J. Moses, 1869.

Breen, T. H., and Stephen Innes. *"Myne Owne Ground": Race and Freedom on Virginia's Eastern Shore, 1640–1676.* New York: Oxford University Press, 1980.

Carretta, Vincent. *Phillis Wheatley: Biography of a Genius in Bondage.* Athens, GA: University of Georgia Press, 2011.

Chicago History Museum. "A New Birth of Freedom: Black Soldiers in the Union Army." https://www.chicagohistory.org/wp-content/uploads/2016/10/CHM-Lincoln-NewBirthofFreedom.pdf.

Cornish, Samuel, and John Russworm. Editorial, *Freedom's Journal* 1 (March 16, 1827), 1. https://web.archive.org/web/20150209163534/http://www.wisconsinhistory.org/pdfs/la/FreedomsJournal/v1n01.pdf.

Cott, Nancy F., et al., eds. *Root of Bitterness: Documents of the Social History of American Women.* 2nd ed. Boston: Northeastern University Press, 1996.

Creel, Margaret Washington. *"A Peculiar People": Slave Religion and Community-Culture Among the Gullahs.* New York: New York University Press, 1988.

Bibliography

Douglass, Frederick. *Douglass' Monthly* 5 (August 1863).

Equiano, Olaudah. *The Interesting Narrative of the Life of Olaudah Equiano, or Gustavus Vassa, the African*. 9th ed. London: By the Author, 1794.

Franklin, John Hope. *From Slavery to Freedom: A History of Negro Americans*. 3rd ed. New York: Alfred A. Knopf, 1967.

Garrison, William Lloyd. "The Insurrection." *The Liberator* 1 (September 3, 1831) 143. http://fair-use.org/the-liberator/1831/09/03/the-liberator-01-36.pdf.

———. "To the Public." *The Liberator* 1 (January 1, 1831) 1. http://fair-use.org/the-liberator/1831/01/01/the-liberator-01-1.pdf.

Gates, Henry Louis, Jr. *The Trials of Phillis Wheatley: America's First Black Poet and Her Encounters with the Founding Fathers*. New York: Basic Civitas, 2003.

Gordon-Reed, Annette. *The Hemingses of Monticello: An American Family*. New York: W. W. Norton, 2008.

Harding, Vincent. *There is a River: The Black Struggle for Freedom in America*. New York: Harcourt Brace Jovanovich, 1981.

Hemings, Madison. "Life Among the Lowly: Recollections of Madison Hemings." *Pike County Republic* (March 13, 1873). https://www.monticello.org/slavery/slave-memoirs-oral-histories/recollections-of-madison-hemings/.

Hening, William Waller, ed. *The Statutes at Large; Being a Collection of All the Laws of Virginia*. Vol. 2. Richmond, VA: Samuel Pleasants, 1810.

Higginbotham, A. Leon, Jr. *In the Matter of Color: Race & The American Legal Process, The Colonial Period*. Oxford: Oxford University Press, 1978.

Higginson, Thomas Wentworth. *Army Life in a Black Regiment*. Boston: Lee and Shepard, 1882. First published 1869.

Jackson, John Andrew. *The Experience of a Slave in South Carolina*. London: Passmore & Alabaster, 1862.

Jefferson, Thomas. *The Papers of Thomas Jefferson Digital Edition*. Edited by James P. McClure and J. Jefferson Looney. Charlottesville: University of Virginia Press, Rotunda, 2008–2021. https://rotunda.upress.virginia.edu/founders/TSJN-01-1-02-160.

Johnson, Charles, and Patricia Smith. *Africans in America: America's Journey Through Slavery*. New York: Harcourt, 1998.

Johnson, Clifton H., ed. *God Struck Me Dead: Voices of Ex-Slaves*. Cleveland: Pilgrim, 1993.

Kolchin, Peter. *American Slavery: 1619–1877*. Rev. ed. New York: Hill and Wang, 2003.

Larson, Kate Clifford. *Bound for the Promised Land: Harriet Tubman, Portrait of an American Hero*. New York: Ballantine, 2004.

Lee, Jarena. *Religious Experience and Journal of Mrs. Jarena Lee*. Rev. ed. Philadelphia: Jarena Lee, 1849.

Levine, Bruce. *The Fall of the House of Dixie: The Civil War and the Social Revolution That Transformed the South*. New York: Random House, 2013.

Marrant, John. *A Narrative of the Lord's Wonderful Dealings with John Marrant, a Black*. 4th ed. London: Gilbert and Plummer, 1785.

Mather, Cotton. *The Negro Christianized: An Essay to Excite and Assist that Good Work, The Instruction of Negro-Servants in Christianity*. Boston: B. Green, 1706.

Mitchell, Henry H. *Black Preaching: The Recovery of a Powerful Art*. Nashville: Abingdon, 1990.

Bibliography

Nash, Gary B. *Red, White, and Black: The Peoples of Early America*. Englewood Cliffs, NJ: Prentice-Hall, 1974.

Occom, Samson. Letter to Susanna Wheatley, 5 March. 1771 MS 771205.1. Dartmouth College. https://collections.dartmouth.edu/occom/html/diplomatic/771205-1-diplomatic.html.

Odell, Margaretta Matilda. *Memoir and Poems of Phillis Wheatley, a Native African and a Slave*. Boston: George W. Light, 1834.

Offley, G. W. *A Narrative of the Life and Labors of the Rev. G. W. Offley, A Colored Man, Local Preacher and Missionary*. Hartford, CT: N.p., 1859.

Painter, Nell Irvin. *Sojourner Truth: A Life, A Symbol*. New York: W. W. Norton, 1996.

Pemberton, Ebenezer. *Heaven the Residence of the Saints*. Boston: E. and C. Dilly, 1771.

Pennington, J. W. C. "The Position and Duties of the Colored People." In *Lift Every Voice: African American Oratory, 1787–1900*, edited by Philip S. Foner and Robert James Branham, 397–407. Tuscaloosa: University of Alabama Press, 1998.

Proper, David R. "Lucy Terry Prince: 'Singer of History.'" *Contributions in Black Studies*, 9 (1990) Article 15. https://scholarworks.umass.edu/cibs/vol9/iss1/15.

Quarles, Benjamin. *Black Abolitionists*. New York: Oxford University Press, 1969.

Raboteau, Albert J. *Slave Religion: The "Invisible Institution" in the Antebellum South*. Updated ed. Oxford: Oxford University Press, 2004.

Shields, John C., ed. *The Collected Works of Phillis Wheatley*. New York: Oxford University Press, 1988.

Slaves' Resistance on Southern Plantations: Selections from the WPA Slave Narratives. National Humanities Center Resource Toolbox, The Making of African American Identity, Vol 1, 1500–1865. http://nationalhumanitiescenter.org/pds/maai/enslavement/text7/resistancewpa.pdf.

Sterling, Dorothy, ed., *We are Your Sisters: Black Women in the Nineteenth Century*. New York: W. W. Norton, 1984.

Stewart, Maria W. *Meditations from the Pen of Mrs. Maria W. Stewart*. Washington, DC: Enterprise, 1879.

Taylor, Susie King. *Reminiscences of My Life in Camp with the 33d United States Colored Troops, Late 1st S.C. Volunteers*. Boston: Published by the author, 1902.

Thompson, L. S. *The Story of Mattie J. Jackson*. Lawrence, MO: Sentinel Office, 1866.

"Time Line of the Civil War." Library of Congress. https://www.loc.gov/collections/civil-war-glass-negatives/articles-and-essays/time-line-of-the-civil-war/.

Truth, Sojourner. *Narrative of Sojourner Truth . . . With a History of Her Labors and Correspondence, Drawn from Her "Book of Life."* Boston: Published for the author, 1875.

Walker, David. *Walker's Appeal, in Four Articles; Together with a Preamble, to the Coloured Citizens of the World, but in Particular, and Very Expressly, to Those of The United States of America*. 3rd ed. Boston: David Walker, 1830.

Ward, Andrew. *The Slaves' War: The Civil War in the Words of Former Slaves*. Boston: Houghton Mifflin Harcourt, 2008.

Wheatley, Phillis. Letter to Mary Wooster, 15 July 1778. Massachusetts Historical Society. https://www.masshist.org/database/772.

———. Letter to Obour Tanner, 19 July 1772. Massachusetts Historical Society. https://www.masshist.org/database/773.

———. Letter to Obour Tanner, 30 October 1773. Massachusetts Historical Society. https://www.masshist.org/database/774.

Bibliography

———. Letter to Obour Tanner, 21 March 1774. Massachusetts Historical Society. http://www.masshist.org/database/775.

———. Letter to Obour Tanner, 29 May 1778. Massachusetts Historical Society. https://www.masshist.org/database/777.

———. Letter to Obour Tanner, 10 May 1779, Massachusetts Historical Society. https://www.masshist.org/database/778.

———. *Poems on Various Subjects, Religious and Moral.* London: A. Bell, 1773.

Wiencek, Henry. *Master of the Mountain: Thomas Jefferson and His Slaves.* New York: Farrar, Straus and Giroux, 2012.

Williams, Peter, Jr. *An Oration on the Abolition of the Slave Trade.* New York: Samuel Wood, 1808.

Index

Adams, Abigail, 9
Adams, John, 9
Africa, xvi, 1, 2, 19, 20, 22, 26, 27, 31, 34, 35, 36, 37, 39, 41, 45, 46, 49, 55, 56, 61, 72, 74, 78, 89, 90, 116, 121
African Awakening, 30–31
African Masonic Hall (Boston, Massachusetts), 89
African Methodist Association (AMA), 60
African Methodist Episcopal Church (AME), 54, 57, 60, 61, 119, 129
Akan, 20
Akron, Ohio, 95
Alabama, 64, 66, 67, 68, 70, 93
Albany, New York, 59
Albert, James (Ukawsaw Gronniosaw), 41
Allah, 23
Allen, Rev. Richard, 53, 54, 55, 57, 58, 74
American Anti-Slavery Society, 80
American Colonization Society (ACS), 55–56
AME Zion Church (Auburn, New York), 119
Anderson, Sister, 58
Andrew, Governor John, 110, 111
Anthony (enslaved African), 24
Antietam, Maryland, 108
Appalachian Mountains, 63–64
Appomattox Courthouse, Virginia, 108
Ardinburgh family, 91
Arkansas, 64, 67
Arlington Heights, Virginia, 117–118

Atlanta, Georgia, 108
Auburn, New York, 102, 106, 119
Augusta, Georgia, 30
Austria, 109

Babylon, 89–90, 122
Bacon, Thomas, 23
Ball, Charles, 66
Baltimore, Maryland, 97, 100
Bantu, 20
Baptists, 15, 20, 28, 29, 30, 84
Battle Creek, Michigan, 96, 117, 121–22
Bell, Mary. *See* Hemings, Mary
Bell, Thomas, 12
Bennett plantation, 3
Berry, Henry, 78–79
Bethel Church of Philadelphia (Bethel AME Church), 54, 55, 56, 57–58, 60
Bethesda (orphanage), 29
Bett, Betsy (Mau Mau), 91
Bibb, Henry, 84
Black Belt, 64, 65, 69–71, 72, 81
Black Loyalists, 30
Black Sal (birthmother), 8, 16
Bomefree, Isabella. *See* Truth, Sojourner
Bomefree, James, 91
Bonaparte, Napoleon, 63
Boston, Massachusetts, 28, 32, 34, 35, 38, 39, 40, 42, 45, 46, 47, 49, 72, 79, 89, 111, 119
Bowery, Charity, 78

Index

Bradford, Sarah H., 90, 103
Brodess, Edward, 97, 98
Brooklyn, New York, xv, 129
Brown, John, 107–8, 113
Brown, Oliver, 107
Brown, Rev. Morris, 60, 62
Brown, Watson, 107
Bryan, Andrew, 30, 54
Buchanan, James, 109n7
Bull Run, 108
Butler, General Benjamin, 111

Caldwell, James, 112
Camp Ward, Detroit, Michigan, 117
Canada, 28, 30, 58, 101, 107, 109
Carey, William, 30
Cary, Richard, 42
Charles II (King), 20
Charleston, South Carolina, 22, 27, 28, 60, 61, 62, 72
Charleston African Association, 60
Charlottesville, Virginia, 12, 14, 15
Chatham, Ontario, 107
Cherokee Indians, 28
Chesapeake Bay, Maryland, 3, 64, 100
Child, Lydia Maria, 111
Church of England, 20, 21, 22, 25
Civil War, ix, xi, 65, 71, 102, 108–10, 120, 122
Clay, Henry, 74
Colored Hospital, Fort Monroe, Virginia, 119
Colored Soldiers' Aid Society, 117
Combahee River, 113, 114, 119
Confederacy, 108, 111, 113, 118
Confederate Constitution, 108
Congo-Angola, 20
Congress, 52, 55, 109, 112, 113, 121
Connecticut, 26, 52
Constitutional Convention, 53
Continental Congress, 7, 9
Cook, James, 97
Cook, Mrs., 97
Cornish, Rev. Samuel, 72
Council for Foreign Plantations, 20
Crissman, Betsy, 66, 87
Crocker, Hannah Mather, 35
Cuffee, Paul, 55

Davis, Jefferson, 105, 108, 117
Dawson, Fannie, 122
Declaration of Independence, 7, 8, 52, 74–75, 79
Deists, 58
Delaware, 54, 112
Detroit, Michigan, 117
Dinah, Aunt, 71
District of Columbia, 68
District of Columbia Emancipation Act of 1862, 116
Dorchester, Massachusetts, 24
Dorchester County, Massachusetts, 96–97
Douglass, Charles, 112
Douglass, Frederick, 80, 90, 96, 103–4, 106, 107, 109, 111, 112
Douglass, Louis, 112
Dred Scott decision, 106
Dumont family, 92, 93, 94
Dunmore, Lord, 8
Dutch Reformed, 20

Eannes de Azurara, Gomes, 20
Edwards, Anderson, 85
Edwards, Jonathan, 26
Elizabeth City County, Virginia, 24
Elk Hill Plantation, 6, 8
Emancipation Proclamation, 105, 108, 112, 113, 117
Episcopalians, 20, 54
Eppes, Elizabeth, 9
Eppes family, 5
Eppes Wayles, Martha, 6
Equiano, Olaudah, 26

Farley, Daniel, 12
54th Massachusetts Infantry, 112
Fillmore, Millard, 109n7
Finley, Robert, 55, 56
First African Baptist Church of Savannah, 30
First Baptist Church of Jamaica, 30
First Church of Deerfield (Massachusetts), 24
First Michigan Colored Infantry Regiment, 117
First South Carolina Volunteer Regiment, 112, 113, 115, 119

Index

Flora (enslaved African), 8
Florida, 119
Forten, James, 56
Fort Monroe, Virginia, 119
Fort Sumter, South Carolina, 108
Fossett, Daniel, 15
Fossett, Edith, 15
Fossett, Isabella, 15
Fossett, Maria, 15
Fossett, Patsy, 15
Fossett, Peter, 15
Fossett, William, 7, 12, 15
Fossett-Hemings, Betsy, 12
Fossett-Hemings, Joseph, 7, 12, 15
France, 9–13, 63, 109
Free African Society, 54
Freedman's Bureau, 118
Freedman's Hospital, 118
Freedman's Village, Arlington, Virginia, 117, 118
Freedom Principle (France), 10, 11
Freedom's Journal, xi, 72–75
Fugitive Slave Act, 101, 106
Fulanis, 20

Galveston, Texas, 113
Gambia, 34
Garnett, Rev. Henry Highland, 105, 106
Garrett, Thomas, 101–2
Garrison, Freeborn, 53
Garrison, William Lloyd, 79–80
General Rules, 29
George, David, 30
Georgia, xv, 22, 27, 30, 41, 52, 53, 67, 68, 81, 108, 116
Gettysburg, 108
Gilbert, Olive, 90
God, x, xii, xiii, xv, 2, 15, 17, 20, 23, 24, 27, 28, 29, 32, 33, 36, 37, 38, 39, 43, 44, 46, 47, 48, 49, 50, 52, 53, 54, 56, 57, 58, 59, 61, 71, 73, 74, 75, 77, 78, 79, 80, 82, 83, 84, 85, 86, 87, 89, 90–94, 95, 96, 98, 99, 101, 102, 103, 104, 111, 113, 116, 122, 123, 128, 130, 131. *See also* Holy Spirit, Jesus Christ
Goose Creek, South Carolina, 25

Gowans, Henry, 70–71
Granger, Archy, 8
Granger, Ursula, 8
Grant, General Ulysses S., 108, 121
Gray, John, 53
Great Awakening, 13, 25, 26–32, 35, 39, 81
Great Britain, 9, 64, 74, 109
Greene, Harriet ("Rit"), 96, 97, 102
Gronniosaw, Ukawsaw (James Albert), 41
Gulf of Mexico, 64

Haiti, 54–55, 63, 116
Hall, Rev., 28
Halleck, General Henry, 111
Hannah (birthmother), 16–17
Harpers Ferry, West Virginia, 107, 108
Harvard University (University of Cambridge), 36, 40
Hastings, Selina (Countess of Huntingdon), 38, 41
Haynes, Leonard, 22
Hemings, Betty Brown, 6
Hemings, Critta, 6
Hemings, Dolly, 6
Hemings, Elizabeth, 5–9, 11–12, 13–14, 15, 16, 19
Hemings, Eston, 12, 14
Hemings, Harriet (2 infants), 12, 14
Hemings, Captain James, 5
Hemings, James (son), 6, 9–11
Hemings, James (grandson), 8
Hemings, John, 7, 13, 14
Hemings, Lucy 7
Hemings, Madison, 5–6, 10–14
Hemings, Martin, 6, 7
Hemings, Mary, 6, 7, 12, 14, 15
Hemings, Molly, 12
Hemings, Nancy, 6
Hemings, Peter, 6
Hemings, Robert, 6, 7
Hemings, Sally, 6, 9–13, 14, 15, 16
Hemings, Thenia, 6
Hemings, William Beverly, 12, 14
Hereditary Slavery Law, 3–4
Hern, Isabel, 9

Index

Higginson, Colonel Thomas Wentworth, 112, 113, 116
Holy Spirit (Holy Ghost), xii, 30, 35, 74, 85
Hook, Peter, 66
Hopkins, Rev. Samuel, 45, 49
Hôtel de Langeac, 9
Hughes, Caroline, 15
Hughes, Wormley, 15
Hunter, General David, 110
hush harbors, 81–82, 84, 85

Igbos, 20
Independence Day, 92
India, 30
Industrial Revolution, 70
Isaac (enslaved preacher), 84
Isabel (enslaved African), 24
Israelites, 29, 54, 61, 82

Jackson, Andrew, 109n7
Jackson, John Andrew, 86–87
Jackson, Mattie, 82
Jacob (enslaved African), 82–83
Jamaica, 30
James River, Virginia, 3, 8
Jamestown, Virginia, 2–3
James VI (King), 2
Jefferson, Lucy Elizabeth, 8, 9, 10
Jefferson, Martha (Patsy), 8, 9, 10, 11, 12
Jefferson, Martha Wayles, 7, 8–9
Jefferson, Mary (Polly), 9, 10, 11
Jefferson, Thomas, 5–17, 53, 63, 109n7
Jesus Christ, xii, xiii, xiv, xvi, 17, 19, 21, 26, 28, 29, 30, 31–32, 37, 44, 49, 57, 59, 63, 69, 73, 74, 81, 82, 83, 85, 86, 94, 95, 96, 103, 121, 122, 128, 130
Johnson, Anthony, 3
Johnson, Mary, 3, 4
Jonah (biblical figure), 57–58
Jones, Absalom, 54
Jones, John R., 15
Joseph (biblical slave), 37

Kansas Territory, 107
Kentucky, 64, 67, 112

Lathrop, Rev. John, 46
Lee, General Robert E., 108, 117
Lee, James, 58
Lee, Jarena, 51, 56–60
Lee, Joseph, 57
Le Jau, Francis, 25
Liberator, The, 79–80
Liberia, 74, 116, 121
Liele, George, 30, 54
Lincoln, Abraham, 106, 108, 109, 111, 113, 114, 116, 117, 120
London, England, 9, 26, 28, 34, 38–42, 43, 44, 45, 46
Louisiana, 63, 64, 66, 67, 68, 75, 83, 111, 112, 119
Louisiana Purchase, 63
Louis X (King), 10
Lutherans, 20, 58

Madison, James, 109n7
Madison, Reuben, 67
Maine, 52
Mansfield Ruling, 42
Marrant, John, 27–28
Martin, Caroline, 68
Martin, Charlotte, 84
Martin, John Sella, 68–69
Martin, Winnifred, 68
Maryland, xiii, xv, 3, 28, 52, 64, 65, 66, 67, 68, 82, 83, 90, 97, 98, 99, 100, 101, 102, 106, 108, 110, 112, 118, 130
Massachusetts, 24, 26, 28, 32, 34, 35, 38, 39, 40, 42, 45, 46, 47, 49, 52, 72, 78, 79, 89, 90, 96–97, 110, 111, 119
Mather, Cotton, 23–24, 35
Mather Crocker, Hannah, 35
Methodism/Methodists, 20, 26, 29, 35, 38, 53, 54, 55, 57, 58, 59, 60, 61
Michigan, 58, 96, 117, 121–22, 130
Middle Passage, 1–2, 31, 34, 36, 37, 49, 64–65. *See also* Second Middle Passage
Militia Act, 112
Miller brothers, 116
Mississippi, 64, 66, 68, 81, 108, 113
Mississippi River, 64

Index

Missouri, 64, 82, 106, 107, 112
Missouri Compromise, 106
Monroe, James, 109n7
Montgomery, Colonel James, 113–14
Monticello, 6, 7, 8, 9, 10, 11, 12, 13, 14, 15, 16
Moss, Andrew, 83

Nantucket, Massachusetts, 90
National American Woman Suffrage Association, 120
National Association of Colored Women, 120
National Freedman's Relief Association, 118
Nealy family, 91–92
New England, 2, 20, 24, 25, 34, 80
New Hampshire, 52
New Jersey, 20, 52, 54, 56, 119
New Orleans, Louisiana, 63, 67, 68, 75
Newport, Rhode Island, 37
New York, ix, xv, 20, 52, 58, 59, 72, 90, 91, 92, 93, 94, 95, 102, 106, 107, 117, 118, 119, 120, 129–130
New York City, New York, ix, xv, 52, 93, 94, 129–130
Nielson, John, 7
Nielson, Joseph, 7
Nielson, Lucy, 7
Norfolk, Virginia, 11
North America, x, xi, 2, 20, 26, 31, 32, 127, 128. *See also specific locations*
North Carolina, 22, 27, 52, 68, 72, 129
North Elba, New York, 107
Northampton, Massachusetts, 26
North Hampton County, Virginia, 3
Nova Scotia, 28, 30

Occom, Rev. Samson, 36, 40, 45–46
Offley, Rev. G. W., 82–83
Ohio, 14, 15, 58, 95
Oklahoma, 65
Old South Church (Boston, Massachusetts), 38, 44
Old State House (Boston, Massachusetts), 34
102nd US Colored Infantry, 117

Oxford University, 26

Paris, France, 9–13
Parisian Admiralty Court, 10
Paul (apostle), 17, 25
Pennington, J. W. C., 113
Pennsylvania, 7, 26, 27, 52, 54, 55, 56, 57, 60, 62, 66, 97, 99, 102
Peter (son of Sojourner Truth), 93, 94
Peter, Jesse, 30
Peters, John, 46–47
Philadelphia, Pennsylvania, 7, 26, 27, 54, 55, 56, 57, 60, 62, 66, 97, 99, 102
Picquet, Louisa, 67
Pierce, Franklin, 109n7
Polk, James K., 109n7
Port Royal, South Carolina, 108, 110, 111, 112
Pottawatomie Creek, 107
Preliminary Emancipation Proclamation, 108
Presbyterians, 20, 36, 56, 58, 59
Prince, Lucy Terry, 24–25
Pritchard, Jack (Gullah Jack), 61
Prosser, Gabriel, 51, 54–55, 61, 80
Prosser, Martin, 54
Providence, Rhode Island, 46
Prussia, 109
Puritans, 20, 23, 26

Quakers, 58, 93, 99, 101
Quomina (enslaved African), 8

Randolph, Thomas Mann, 12
religious revivals, 16, 19–32, 35, 39, 81
Revolutionary War, 8, 13, 26, 30, 32, 43, 46, 47, 49, 52, 54, 55, 64
Reynolds, Katherine, 84
Reynolds, Mary, 83–84
Rhode Island, 37, 46
Richmond, Virginia, 54, 122
Ross, Araminta. *See* Tubman, Harriet
Ross, Ben, 98
Ross, Benjamin, 96, 102
Ross, Henry, 98
Rowe, Levi, 93
Russworm, John, 72

Index

Said, Omar Ibn, 22
Savannah, Georgia, 27, 30, 116
Savannah River, 30
Saxton, General Rufus, 112, 119
Scott, Dred, 106
Scott, General Winfield, 111
Scott, Harriet, 106
Scott, Jesse, 15
Scott, William, 57
Scriver, Mr., 92
Sea Islands, 108
Second Middle Passage, 63–71, 80, 81. *See also* Middle Passage
Second South Carolina Infantry, 113
Sharpe, Granville, 42
Sherman, General Tecumseh, 108
Shiloh, Tennessee, 108
Sierra Leone, 55
Silver Bluff Baptist Church (South Carolina), 30
Skelton, Elizabeth Lomax, 6
Smith, James, 81
Smith, Mr., 59
Snow Hill, Pennsylvania, 57
Society for the Propagation of the Gospel in Foreign Parts (SPG), 22, 25
Society of Negros, 24
South Carolina, 22, 25, 27, 28, 30, 52, 53, 60, 62, 68, 72, 74, 86, 108, 110, 112, 113, 115, 119
Spain, 109
Springfield First African Baptist Church (Augusta, Georgia), 30
Stewart, Maria, 89–90, 122
St. George's Methodist Church, 54
Stoughton, Rev., 24
Stowe, Harriet Beecher, 90, 94–95, 96, 102
St. Philip's African Episcopal Church (Philadelphia, Pennsylvania), 52
Sumner, General Edwin, 111
Supreme Court, 106, 109
Susan, Miss, 97

Taney, Chief Justice Robert Brooke, 106
Tanner, Obour, 35, 37, 42, 44, 45, 47, 49
Taylor, Susie King, 115–16, 119, 120
Taylor, Zachary, 109n7
Tennessee, 64, 66, 108, 112
Texas, 113
The Liberator, 79–80
13th Amendment, 113
Thomas (husband of Sojourner Truth), 92, 94
Thomas, Rev. Samuel, 25
Thompson, Anthony, 97
Thornton, John, 43, 44–45, 46
Tilly (enslaved African), 100–101
Titus, Frances, 90
Tonies Vineyard, 3
Trail of Tears, 64–65
Truth, Sojourner (Isabella Bomefree), 90, 91–96, 104, 105, 112, 117–18, 120–21, 122
Tubman, Harriet (Araminta Ross), 90, 91, 96–104, 105, 106, 107–8, 109, 110–16, 119–20, 122
Tubman, John, 98, 99
Tufton (Jefferson farm), 12
Turner, Nat, 77–78
Turner's revolt, 77–80
Twenty-Fifth Corps, United States Colored Troops, 122
Tyler, John, 109n7

Ulster County, New York, 91
Underground Railroad, 15, 89, 96–104
Union, 64, 107, 108, 110, 111, 112, 115, 116, 118, 119, 123
Union Army, 108, 110, 111, 112, 113–14, 115, 116, 120, 122
United States, x, xi, xii, xv, xvi, 5, 13, 16, 26, 51, 52, 55, 56, 59, 61, 62, 63–64, 65, 72–73, 74, 75, 89–90, 106, 108, 109, 111, 112, 113, 116, 118, 120, 123, 130. *See also specific locations*
United States Colored Troops, 122
University of Cambridge (Harvard University), 36

Van Buren, Martin, 109n7
Van Wagener family, 93–94
Vassa, Gustavus (Olaudah Equiano), 26

Index

Vermont, 52
Vesey, Denmark, 51, 61, 62, 80
Virginia, 2–5, 6, 9, 11, 12, 14, 15, 16, 21, 24, 28, 52, 54, 65, 66, 67, 68, 70, 77, 78, 79, 81, 107, 108, 111, 112, 117, 118, 119, 122
Virginia Company of London, 2
Virginia House of Burgesses, 22
Virginia Slave Codes, 4

Walker, David, 64, 72–75, 77, 79
Walker's *Appeal*, 64, 72–75, 77, 79
Washington, DC, x, 117, 118, 120, 121
Washington, George, 55, 109n7
Watson, A. P., 65n4
Wayles, John, 6
Wayles, Martha Eppes, 6
Wesley, Charles, 26
Wesley, John, 26, 29
West Virginia, 107, 108

Wheatley, John, 34, 39–40, 46
Wheatley, Mary, 35, 46
Wheatley, Nathaniel, 35, 42, 46
Wheatley, Phillis, 32, 33–50
Wheatley, Sarah, 35
Wheatley, Susanna, 34–35, 38, 42, 43, 46, 47, 48
Whitefield, George, 26–29, 30, 32, 35, 38–42
William (enslaved African), 24
Williams, Peter, Jr., 52
Williams, Rev. Richard, 57–58
Williamsburg, Virginia, 5
Wilmington, North Carolina, 72
Woman's Rights Convention, 95
Wooster, General David, 44n25, 49
Wooster, Mary, 49

YMCA, 110
Yorubas, 20

www.ingramcontent.com/pod-product-compliance
Lightning Source LLC
Chambersburg PA
CBHW022124160426
43197CB00009B/1141